ZERO SPACE

ZERO SPACE

MOVING

BEYOND

ORGANIZATIONAL

LIMITS

Frank Lekanne Deprez
René Tissen

BERRETT–KOEHLER PUBLISHERS, INC.
San Francisco

Berrett-Koehler Publishers, Inc.
235 Montgomery Street, Suite 650
San Francisco, CA 94104-2916
Tel: (415) 288-0260 Fax: (415) 362-2512 www.bkconnection.com

Ordering Information
Quantity sales. Special discounts are available on quantity purchases by corporations, associations, and others. For details, contact the "Special Sales Department" at the Berrett-Koehler address above.
Individual sales. Berrett-Koehler publications are available through most bookstores. They can also be ordered direct from Berrett-Koehler: Tel: (800) 929-2929; Fax: (802) 864-7626; www.bkconnection.com
Orders for college textbook/course adoption use. Please contact Berrett-Koehler: Tel: (800) 929-2929; Fax: (802) 864-7626.
Orders by U.S. trade bookstores and wholesalers. Please contact Publishers Group West, 1700 Fourth Street, Berkeley, CA 94710. Tel: (510) 528-1444; Fax: (510) 528-3444.

Berrett-Koehler and the BK logo are registered trademarks of Berrett-Koehler Publishers, Inc.

Printed in the United States of America
Berrett-Koehler books are printed on long-lasting acid-free paper. When it is available, we choose paper that has been manufactured by environmentally responsible processes. These may include using trees grown in sustainable forests, incorporating recycled paper, minimizing chlorine in bleaching, or recycling the energy produced at the paper mill.

Library of Congress Cataloging-in-Publication Data
Lekanne Deprez, Frank
　　Zero space : moving beyond organizational limits / Frank Lekanne Deprez and René Tissen.
　　　　p. cm.
　　Includes bibliographical references and index.
　　ISBN 1-57675-182-1
　　1. Communication in rganizations.　2. Management—Communication systems.
I. Tissen, René Johannes, 1955–　II. Title.

HD30.3 .D465 2002
658—dc21 　　　　　　　　　　　　　　　　　　　　　　2002018374

First Edition
07　06　05　04　03　02　　　　　　　　10　9　8　7　6　5　4　3　2　1

Interior Design & Illustration: Gopa Design & Illustration
Copy Editor: Sandra Beris　　　　　　　　　Indexer: Paula C. Durbin-Westby
Proofreader: Henrietta Bensussen　　　　　Production: Linda Jupiter, Jupiter Productions

CONTENTS

PREFACE

■ ■ ■ ■ ■ ■ ■ ■

N<small>O MORE LIMITS.</small> Can it be true? We believe it is. Take a look around you. We are witnessing the end of the organization as we know it. We are moving toward a time when organizations mean . . . well, nothing. Just as knowledge flows faster than business's ability to capture it, so innovative businesses evolve faster than their managers' ability to imagine new and more suitable organizational forms.

We are moving into an age when zero rules. In the old economy, zero meant nothing; in the knowledge-based economy it means everything. We talk about zero stocks, zero lead time, zero response time, zero emissions. For many companies these terms define the future; for others, they pose a seemingly insurmountable threat to the very foundations of business thinking. Cutting-edge Internet companies say the revolution has already been won; companies still anchored in traditional business environments ask themselves who these upstarts really are. Enthusiasts say the future is already here; skeptics feel they are being forced to leap before they have had a chance to look.

Change, it would seem, is not only far more rapid than at any other time in business history but also far more radical. Much of today's change is due to new insights into the true wealth of a company. Tangible assets— the bastions of the old economy—are becoming less important and there is a new awareness of the significance of intangible assets. The value of a company no longer derives from stocks, machinery, and buildings but rather from knowledge, competencies, patents, and client focus. This shift is clearly illustrated by the growing disparity between declared book value and the value the market places on a company. When Steven Spielberg, Jeffrey Katzenberg, and David Geffen started DreamWorks the company had declared assets of $250 million, but the market valued the company's shares at $2 billion.[1] Successful companies—those valued highly in the markets of the world—are realizing that they must not only gain value in physical space but also create wealth in virtual space.

In the knowledge-based economy, however, nothing is black and white. There is no clear demarcation between the real and virtual worlds. Even the most dedicated virtual operation must at some time enter the real world. Most goods and services remain tangible products, and ultimately they must reach real-world customers. The true challenge for managers is to understand the changes and approach them with an open mind, in every aspect of their business.

ALL-BRAIN, NO-BODY ORGANIZATIONS IN ACTION

Donna Dubinsky, coinventor of the Palm Pilot and founder and CEO of Handspring (www.handspring.com) says: "Our company outsources as much as it possibly can—all manufacturing and distribution, for example, gets done elsewhere—in order to keep its innovative core as small as possible. When I joined Apple in 1981, I was employee number 2,588, and we were doing just over $200 million in annualized sales. At Handspring, we hit $200 million in annualized sales with about 250 employees. In other words, today you can do the same business with one-tenth of the staff."[2]

It's the all-brain processes that add value to a company. They are the intangible assets that make up a company's weightless wealth.

And just as organizations will have to exist in less tangible, less prescribed forms, so will our thinking. We have traditionally allowed ourselves to think in boxes, in compartmentalized, sealed territories. Unless we clear our minds of such ideas—ideas that cage us into the past—we can never hope to spread our wings and fly.

BEFORE MEMORY

In Zen no meaning is great meaning, and great meaning is no meaning. We call this zero mind. I go around and ask, "Is zero a number?" One time in London I asked this, and somebody said, "Yes, it's a number."

So I said, "If you say zero is a number, you can do everything. Let's look at this: $9 \times 0 = 0$. Then, $9 = 0/0$. OK? If you say it's a number, then $0/0 = 1$. So $9 = 0/0 = 1$, and $9 = 1$."

Then he said, "Ah, zero is not a number; that's not possible. To get $0/0 = 1$ is not possible."

"OK, not possible is OK. Then, $9 \times 0 = 0$. That means $9 = 0/0$. And $10,000 \times 0 = 0$. Then $10,000 = 0/0$. Then $0/0$ means $0/0 = 10,000$ and $0/0 = 9$. So $9 = 10,000$.

"Zero mind can do anything. If you say zero is a number, that's OK. If you say zero is not a number, that's OK. It doesn't matter. Zero is everything; everything is zero. This is Zen mathematics. So zero mind is very interesting. If you keep zero mind, then you can do everything."[3]

Why We Wrote This Book

When the dot-com bubble burst, managers and entrepreneurs stopped talking about the distant future and started talking about "just" tomorrow. Gone was the desire to make grand plans; instead, managers became content to dream small dreams. They allowed themselves to return to business as usual, in the sense that they reached for the management tools they had been using for decades. The result was centralization, concentration, owning, and "hire-and-fire" policies. In our opinion, this was a vast step backwards.

So we developed a concept to help managers move forward once again. The concept, which we call *zero space*, allows people to leave their comfort zones and get past the limits in organizations.

■ They will understand the complexity of today's organizations and their limitations to continued success.

■ They will reexamine preconceived notions about what makes an organization successful.

■ They will go beyond the quick fix on organizational issues and focus on the architecture of the organization, its boundaries, and its people.

■ They will design and imagine an organizational approach that suits them and their business.

Audience

This book is intended for CEOs, managers, and consultants who are constantly challenged to move beyond organizational limits—create less interference, demolish "walls," and eliminate barriers in order to (dis)organize for success. Only when people are challenged and move outside the comfort zone—and break through to the other side!—can they operate confidently and successfully in zero space.

Acknowledgments

We are grateful to many people. First and foremost, we are indebted to Raymond Yeh, Keri Pearson, and George Kozmetsky, whose zero time concept inspired us to ask ourselves the crucial question: "Just how zero-minded can you get?"[4] We had to clear our minds of all barriers and take a giant step.

Yeh, Pearson, and Kozmetsky paved the way for twenty-first century companies to become zero time companies: "Just being faster is not enough. To win, we must see differently and act instantly. We must operate in zero time."[5] But we believe that our concept of zero space provides a more achievable step toward an integrated perspective on new organizational forms for company success. Apart from adding some—in our view fundamental—"zeros" to the zero time concept, we have made an attempt to create a transparent model that can be applied today.

In our journey into zero space we were extremely lucky that Jonathan Ellis—an outstanding professional and a true confidant—was willing to join us and be our guardian angel in our quest to "boldly go where no man has gone before." It is rare to come across a person as unique as Jonathan.

Our thanks must also be extended to Jim Lee of CTTS Information Services, Los Angeles, who helped with our section on the emergence of Internet communities in chapter 15.

Many others helped in the preparation of this book, including our colleagues at KPMG Knowledge Advisory Services, the incomparable Joie van Tilburg-Rose, Pepi Rozendaal, and many other colleagues. We especially thank our friends in KPMG's IRC unit for actively chasing down the information, articles, and other references that we needed.

We dedicate this book to our partners Petra and Marie-José, who provide us the caring, sharing family community that we need to thrive in zero space, and our children Hidde, Siebe, Jeroen, Marlies, Matthijs, Ceder, and most recently Wicky, who continue to enrich our lives. We also wish to remember Piet van Rooijen of Noordwijk, the Netherlands for his lifelong friendship.

Finally, we are indebted to our agent Hans Ritman, our publisher Steven Piersanti, five critical reviewers, our editor Sandra Beris, and all our friends at Berrett-Koehler for their creative and constructive but sometimes frustrating suggestions.

We have benefited from the writings of other observers of the business scene, whose efforts are annotated in the text. It is truly inspiring to work among such great professionals and innovators.

Frank Lekanne Deprez
René Tissen
March 2002
Amsterdam, The Netherlands

INTRODUCTION:
TIME TO BREAK OUT

WE ARE TRAPPED, caught in a prison of our own making, unable to operate effectively, get things done, or get our people to work together, unable to release the true potential that we know our companies contain.

It's not a nice place to be, this prison. It inhibits our freedom. It forces us to focus on the inside. It keeps the outside at a distance.

The name of this prison? Quite simply: the organization.

We all know how organizations have developed to meet new market needs. Divisions, departments, business units, operating companies, national sales units have been created. All have had their uses. All were developed to make our companies more competitive, more streamlined, more rational, more profitable.

But now the organizations we created have become tyrants. They have taken control, holding us fettered, creating barriers that hinder rather than help our businesses. The lines that we drew on our neat organizational diagrams have turned into walls that no one can scale or penetrate or even peer over.

For most of us who have been in companies with a history longer than five minutes, the freewheeling spirit of the dot-com organization seems far removed from the darkness of our prison. We understand that new technology, a new approach to doing business, allows such companies to run their operations unfettered by the complicated structures that still exist in much of the business world.[1] "It's all very well for them," we sigh, "but they don't have to fight all the interdepartmental battles that we have to fight." And that's true. "If only we were starting a company now," we sigh.

But in business, "if-onlies" simply don't count. Most of us have to work with what we have, not what we wish we had—if only. So what can we—managers caught up in existing organizations—do to address the new challenges presented by the knowledge-based economy?

Often books such as this one seem to assume that its readers are starting off with a clean slate. Or they seem to suggest that it is necessary to throw the baby out with the bathwater. That's not what we are suggesting. We understand that existing organizations cannot change overnight. Many are rooted in a long tradition, with established hierarchies, and lines of authority and communication. But these should not be used as excuses for inaction.

The organizational concept of zero space aims to help existing companies understand the requirements of the knowledge-based economy and the changes in structure and mentality they need to make in order to compete with the companies that do start without all the baggage.

Taking a Look at the Other Side

Here's an interesting explanation of the extent of the universe. Imagine flying in a spaceship until you can go no farther. There you discover that the outer limit of our infinite universe is actually a brick wall. This is where the universe ends, you are told. You look at the wall and one question pops into your mind: What's on the other side?

Organizations have boundaries every bit as tangible as brick walls. But very few people operating in these organizations ever ask that one question.

Why not?

The question is simple, the answer complex. Many organizations place too much emphasis on individual and functional goals and too little on what's outside. Boundaries between units arise naturally as different units—units of one, groups, teams, networks, communities, organizations, nations—pursue different objectives and therefore develop a license to operate that is often difficult to imitate. It is impractical to expect people to behave as if these boundaries do not exist.

Many organizations today are still firmly grounded in the industrial past. They have evolved against a background of mature markets, complex industrial processes, and five-year business plans. Hierarchical, cumbersome, inflexible, and lethargic, they are the dinosaurs of business. The recent Internet failures have made many of these old dinosaurs believe that their model is the winner, but is it? In the knowledge-based economy, business dinosaurs may make a great noise but they will find it difficult to make a profit. The speed of innovation, shortened product cycles, complexity of offerings required by an increasingly demanding consumer—all mean that organizations must be "all brains and no body." Nonbrain weight should be kept to an absolute minimum, all such processes outsourced or eliminated entirely. It's the all-brain processes that add value to a company. They are the intangible assets that make up its weightless wealth that remains essential today—despite the experience of the failed dot-coms.

Asking the Big Question

So how do we break out of our organizational prisons? The first step is to ask the question, "What's on the other side?" This means applying our natural curiosity to our business.

Many of our companies' limits are not built with bricks. They are not tangible structures. They cannot be pointed out. And they cannot be knocked down with a sledgehammer. Many of the limits are simply in our minds. We create them, maintain them, give them an indestructibility they do not actually have. And if they exist only in our minds, then that is the place we have to clear first.

"Oh, sure," you are probably saying, "It's all right for you to talk—you don't have to face the fights, the obstructions, the difficulties that I have to face every day."

That's where you're wrong. We fight the same battles as you do, every single day. We deal with a lack of cooperation, a lack of sharing. We deal with inflexibility, indecisiveness, an inability to get things done now—rather than in six weeks' time. We deal with all the things that any manager, anywhere, has to deal with.

But we also know that these problems won't go away unless we ask the question. Because asking that simple question—"What's on the other side?"—is the first step toward obtaining the greatest weapon possible: zero-mindedness.

Becoming Zero-Minded

Nelson Mandela reportedly said that although his political opponents could imprison his body, they could never imprison his mind. And yet many of us in business allow our minds to be imprisoned in old-time, industrial age thinking. We tell ourselves that things were always done this way. The organization was designed to help business. Divisions are natural. It makes economic sense for each division or unit—or whatever you choose to call it—to be regarded as an individual profit center.

Yet deep down we know that we are fooling ourselves. Our rigid organizational structures prevent close cooperation between people who may be doing the same work but are located in different departments or even, as globalization increases, on different continents. Organizational and geographical borders have conspired to keep us trapped.

We've allowed ourselves to become victims of the tyranny of the pigeon-hole.

Becoming zero-minded means letting go of the restricting preconceptions, emptying your mind of the barriers that exist there, and learning to ask: "What's on the other side?"

Scope of the Book

Part I deals more closely with the concepts of zero space and zero-mindedness. Matter matters less in today's world, where companies are changing and intangibles rule. Zero-mindedness means freeing oneself from one's imagined cell and dealing with the real world as it is today.

Part II discusses the eight features of zero space—eight zeroes. Each one is based on practical conflicts that businesses face, conflicts caused by needing to move faster, with less baggage, without constantly encountering resistance.

If we were honest, we would all acknowledge that it often takes too much time to get things done. Large organizations are like mammoth tankers: the pilot can change course but it takes a long time for the tanker to respond. In today's world there's simply not enough time to wait for that change of course. We have to trade in our tankers for tugboats—nippy little workmanlike vessels that can zip in and out of a harbor in no time.

But there's more to a tugboat than speed. There's strength too, strength to pull an idea into port. And a readiness to do this with whatever vessel is waiting. Tugboats see nothing wrong in pulling a tanker one minute and a liner the next. They are prepared to work with any ship around. Because working with others is what their business is about.

In contrast, in corporate life, a "good guys, bad guys" mentality lingers. Needless to say, we all consider ourselves one of the good guys. Yet in the knowledge-based economy there cannot be good guys and bad guys but only useful and trustful "guys and girls." Part of becoming zero-minded is no longer pigeonholing companies as friends or foes. People used to say you have to go where the money is; today companies have to go where the knowledge is. It's no longer a question of owning knowledge but rather of making use of knowledge to add value. You're expanding into a new market? Why build up your own distribution and logistics operation when you can make use of one—probably a lot better than yours, anyway—that is run by logistics specialists? After all, if your car needs a can of oil, you go out and buy one—you don't start drilling your own well!

YAHOO VERSUS GANNETT

Gannett, a diversified U.S. media concern, owns the national newspaper USA Today, a slew of local newspapers, and twenty-two television stations in mostly secondary and tertiary markets. Yahoo is an Internet portal through which nearly two hundred million people around the world pass every month.

In 1999, Yahoo's market capitalization was roughly five times that of Gannett. In 2001, Gannett's market capitalization was roughly twice that of Yahoo. Put another way, two years ago, Yahoo could have acquired Gannett with relative ease. Now Gannett would be the more likely to acquire. The question is: Why doesn't it? Gannett is a solid, well-managed company. It delivers a steady profit, operating its various properties at high margins—between 17 percent and 35 percent—while rigorously controlling costs. But its growth prospects are constrained by the nature of the business it's in. It still has to buy roll after roll of newsprint. It still has to run printing plants all around the country. It still has to operate huge fleets of trucks. And although many of its news properties run Web sites, Internet companies continue to attack its most important advertising revenue stream: classified advertising.[2]

This idea—that you no longer have to own knowledge—is frightening to many people. They believe it compromises their business, puts them at the mercy of a competitor. But being zero-minded means being ready to break bread with your enemies, sit down with them, talk to them, share with them.

One of the most moving business events in the aftermath of September 11, 2001, was the decision of the New York Stock Exchange to offer office space—and access to its confidential systems—to its archrival, the American Stock Exchange. For many people such an action had been unthinkable, but in the wake of the Twin Towers disaster, traditional competitors realized that cooperation was the name of the new game in town.

The eight zeroes of zero space are all logical. They do not require a gigantic reengineering process, only a new mentality.

Finally, Part III offers some practical ideas about how to launch into zero space, how to apply the eight zeroes to your own business, to understand how flexibility is the key attribute of knowledge-based companies.

Today, knowledge is the currency. The challenge to business is to leverage the knowledge within, create knowledge-expanding alliances, and create new knowledge that can be turned into profit-making products and services.

Tangible assets have had their day; intangibles now rule. Ideas and actionable knowledge are valuable. In his book *Accidental Genius*, Mark Levy writes: "Companies worth millions—Millions? Hell, billions!—are somehow leveraging their smarts, their imaginations, and are ringing registers worldwide by bringing their head-built products to market. Take Microsoft, for instance. Here's a company with $1.5 billion in hard assets, yet it has a market value of over $318 billion. That means the 'invisibles' of the company—'goodwill,' perceived brand value, and the thoughts percolating in Bill Gates's noggin—are worth three hundred times the company's 'touchables.'"[3]

But where, you may ask, do all these ideas reside? You got it—inside the heads of employees, the people who make up a company. There's no way a company can own what's inside people's heads. If they decide to leave, all that knowledge and power walks out the door with them.

If there's one area where zero-mindedness has to be employed to break the tyranny of the pigeonhole, it is in the relationships companies maintain with their employees. This is why we deal with a major transformation taking place—the move away from *human resource management* toward *people relationship management.*

Ultimately, people have the ideas that make a company successful. It is the manager's task to ensure that people feel happy and comfortable enough to release those ideas. It means that their main task, once again, will be to manage people. For they are the lifeblood of a company.

Zero Space Awaits You

We are not promising an easy journey into zero space. But we are promising an exciting, rewarding journey. Once you break through all the limits—physical and mental—that keep your company trapped, you will be able to start leveraging the knowledge you already have to build a sustainable and successful company.

How long will it take? We cannot set a time limit. Indeed, we wonder if there is any final destination! For we do not believe that our universe ends at a brick wall—we are, after all, zero-minded. But we do know that only companies that understand the full value of zero will be able to navigate the streams of business in the knowledge-based economy.

Clear your mind of all barriers and all preconceived ideas. Allow yourself to move into the knowledge-based economy. Allow yourself to discover the liberation of zero space, where you can alternate between two states of existence: a *matter* state and a *space* state. Zero-mindedness stimulates the imagination to find new possibilities for overcoming limits. It gives people the courage to create new organizational forms that suit them and their organizations. Finally, it drives people to move others beyond their personal comfort zone without making them uncertain.

If we are to zero in on the future, then we must take a giant step into zero space. So come with us on a journey into infinite potential.

PART I

The Power of Zero Mindedness

1

ZERO RULES

■ ■ ■ ■ ■ ■ ■ ■ ■ ■ ■

MARKETPLACES ARE CHANGING. Even our definition of doing business is changing. And unless organizations change too, their chance of success decreases by the minute. This is something fundamentally different from the reorganizing that many companies did too much of in the past. The focus is now on sustainable growth and unlimited potential.

Moving the Organization into the Knowledge-Based Economy

Traditionally, a company involved a number of employees who worked in a series of corporate buildings and supplied a product or a service in a well-defined marketplace. Today, that is no longer how companies are defined. They are in constant flux, looking for new ways to add value anytime, anyplace, anywhere. And it is obvious that this new fluidity cannot be put into an old organizational bottle.

The most significant reason for this change is the move to the knowledge-based economy. Knowledge-intensive companies are no longer the exception; they are the norm. And knowledge companies find that they cannot hem themselves into traditional buildings and rigid organizational structures. Today's business possibilities seem endless—and so do the work possibilities. With the rapid dissemination of IT, professionals are no longer bound by time or space. The twenty-four-hour economy has made the former archaic; working on-line or off-line has made the latter meaningless. Mobile phones, laptops, Internet access, e-mail, these are far more important in the knowledge-based economy than are buildings or desks.

Although some people thrive on such unlimited possibilities, others—perhaps most—feel threatened by them. They are afraid that they will lose their sense of belonging, that they will soon be working for a company with no true identity. They fear that they will simply float across some endless, uncharted sea. The fear of isolation increases, and they have nothing tangible on which to rely. The boundaries that have long prescribed their world are disintegrating. The traditional divisions—insourcing and outsourcing, lines of authority and responsibility—are becoming so vague as to be virtually irrelevant.

Some fear that if the boundaries are removed, the company will cease to exist. For, they maintain, boundaries define the company. But today's business environment does not allow for comfort; boundaries must be constantly questioned, redefined, and transcended. So the question that must be answered is this: Where does an organization start and where does it end?

As former labor secretary R. B. Reich wrote, the challenge for management today is to turn old-line companies into on-line companies.[1] The Greek philosopher Heraclitus once said that you could never step in the same stream twice. Today, the stream of business is becoming a torrent, sweeping companies forward. They may not know where they're going, but they do know there is no benefit in trying to fight the currents.

For many years, management concentrated on the business of relations: *customer relations, public relations, employee relations.* All were aimed at one thing: maintaining the status quo. Any disturbances—whether internal or external—had to be eliminated, any turbulence had to be calmed. Reich calls those who manage these relations *heat shields.*

"Think of them as heat shields," he writes, "who dampen, deflect, or moderate the demands coming from inside and outside the organization, telling the company that it has to change. In the knowledge-based economy, heat shields, who think that they are the company's staunchest defenders, become the company's worst enemies—by protecting it too well from demanding customers, clients, and constituents."[2]

Heat shields, like boundaries, can no longer be tolerated. Although it may have been possible for them to protect a company's tangible assets, they have little effect on intangibles. Knowledge, information, ideas, and concepts all flow freely, ignoring artificial barriers.

Yet if companies traditionally gained their identity by setting up bound-aries—between themselves and the competition, between one market-place and another, between one department, division, or even business unit and another—and guaranteed their ability to function by creating rigid organizational structures, how will they work in a world in which the very scaffolding of structure is being dismantled?

A TRUE SHIFT?

The industrial revolution occurred when we stopped using agrarian mod-els to run the agrarian and industrial sectors. However, the industrial model did not push the farmer model off the stage. Rather, it merely joined the agrarian model in the limelight.[3]

In the same way that technologies evolve faster than a business's abili-ties to absorb them, businesses evolve faster than their managers' abilities to develop new and more suitable organizational forms. And so we repeat the question: Where does an organization start and where does it end?

The answer is in *zero space*. In zero space, all matter—whether tangi-ble or intangible, large or small—is linked. Value networks exist at every level. Such networks—fluid, adaptable, changeable, challenging—replace the rigid structures of the old industrial thinking.

So is zero space a void, a vacuum, in which there is a total lack of control?

M. J. Hatch uses improvisational jazz as powerful metaphor to describe empty space in organizations. Although there is a harmonic structure, it does not restrict the performers but rather frees them. It is a structure that supports but does not specify. Jazz musicians never accept the status quo; the structure is there for them as a guideline but they want to investigate the freedom, not the restrictions. In jazz, *not* playing structures—just allowing the structures to remain implied, a basis—creates the space a musician needs to improvise in.[4]

QUANTUM THINKING: VISION THINKING IN PRACTICE

"Quantum thinking is creative, insightful, intuitive thinking. It is the kind of thinking with which we challenge our assumptions, break our habits, or change our mental models, our paradigms. It is the kind of thinking that invents new categories of thought, that creates new patterns and new language. . . .

"Quantum thinking has the capacity to question itself and to question the environment. It is called into play when the unexpected happens, in situations of crisis or opportunity when our rule-bound and habit-bound thinking can't cope. It is being able to see that existing categories don't work, being able to put those categories on hold, and then being able to create new categories, some of which involve new meaning. It is our ability to do this kind of thinking that makes us *truly human*, and it arises from the deepest recesses of the self. But using this ability requires that we step outside our usual thinking or usual paradigm. It requires that we gain a further perspective from which we can see the thinking behind our thinking."[5]

For companies in the knowledge-based economy, structure or organization must become implicit rather than explicit. There must be room for intuitive thinking, for a spontaneity that enables organizational members to anticipate and proactively sense the opportunities that depend to a large extent on their ability to improvise. The organization must create space that allows for flights of fancy and creativity. Creativity is a natural function of the mind, as natural as breathing.[6] Thinking outside the box, where there is room for surprises and creativity, will determine the structure; strategy, which largely depends on a strict plotting of events, will no longer be something planned in advance but rather something that evolves naturally. After all, how do you chart a path through unknown territory?

According to Richard D'Aveni, professor of strategic management at Dartmouth College, "Say Lewis and Clark want to go West. They know there is a general direction of progress for their industry. That's all they know. So they climb the first hill and when they get to the top they look around and point to the next hill in the general direction and say to themselves: 'That looks reasonably easy to climb,' and they set off in that direction. Is it the most efficient way to move? To find a path from one hill to another? Most probably not. But in the end they stumble onto things that they most probably wouldn't have come across if they had got a map and planned the shortest path from A to B."[7]

In today's rapidly changing times, we sometimes feel that we are not only in uncharted territory but also surrounded by a thick mist. Signposts loom up before us; we must be flexible enough to change direction at the shortest notice. But that is virtually impossible if our companies are straitjacketed into strict, formal hierarchies.

Zero space offers freedom of movement, freedom of operation, freedom to allow fantasy to take us into new territories where we can achieve our business goal of adding value.

Sharing Space

Just as organizational boundaries are becoming increasingly blurred, so too are the boundaries between market areas. Companies no longer compete in clearly defined market areas but rather in abstract space. The old concepts of personal space, of invading space, will be relegated to the past. In their place must come the awareness that no company will ever again be able to dominate one area of business space. No company can "own" space; all have to learn to share it. Mahanbir Sawhney, professor of electronic commerce and technology at Northwestern University, and David Parikh, management consultant at PRTM, Silicon Valley, write, "The Net has destroyed the old lines dividing businesses, markets, industries, and geographies."[8]

As companies transform themselves into zero space organizations the true challenge is not just to exist in that space but also actively to share it. Intangibles—knowledge, ideas, concepts—are the new corporate assets. Ideas have never recognized borders. Concepts have always leaped continents. And knowledge is more swiftly disseminated throughout the world today than at any time in our history.

Any organizational structure must recognize this free flow of ideas. While ensuring as much as possible that these intangibles first add value to the company's own operations (that is, after all, the very reason for being in business), it must also eliminate the constraints that can impede the flow between people operating in the same space.

Many companies have been persuaded that networks, whether electronic or personal, are the answer to all their problems. And indeed, networks can engender a feeling of belonging. But if they are to be successful, they must be accessible to everyone. The danger that we are constantly seeing is that such networks are used to *share* an experience rather than to create a *shared* experience. The difference is not just a play on words; it is a fundamental attitude that must be addressed very seriously indeed.

Zero space organizations operate independently of time, geography, and matter. They help define the shared space in which knowledge, people, and technology can constantly combine and recombine. They provide ever-changing, ever-evolving connections that are the basis for a shared experience.

ZERO REAL ESTATE: THE PLATFORM OF SPACE

Michael J. Young is managing partner of global real estate programs for Accenture, a global provider of management and technology consulting services and solutions. He writes: "We no longer think of real estate. We think of creating the platform of space, technology, and services that people need. Work is not where you are, it's what you do."[9]

2

The Currency of
Zero Space

■ ■ ■ ■ ■ ■ ■ ■ ■ ■

Two friends meet for a drink. As they leave the bar, one of them realizes he has no cash on him. His friend gives him $10 for his cab fare home. So now that friend has $10 less while the other has $10 more. During their evening together, the two shared a lot of thoughts. One friend told the other about an idea of his, and the other did the same. Now both friends are one idea richer, but neither is an idea poorer.

Sharing knowledge enriches people, and it also enriches companies. It is a situation in which one plus one is always infinitely more than two. So companies must allow ideas and knowledge to move freely, for then this knowledge can multiply and add value.

But many managers still believe that knowledge withheld is power. So companies in which knowledge is shared freely must prove that they have the advantage over those that hoard or hide it. Furthermore, they must understand when to share and when not to share knowledge.

Sharing knowledge is a critical business success factor because it raises the level of quality thinking. But in any organizational setting—whether off-site or on-site, off-line or on-line, physical or virtual—the longer knowledge has been around, the less valuable it usually is. The so-called decay factor makes knowledge stale, out of date, obsolete, superseded, or even incorrect.[1] Every individual's knowledge is strongly challenged by the decay factor. The sell-by date of certain professional knowledge (about stocks, information technology, people) is extremely short. That's why a brain-connecting approach that focuses on freely communicating valuable knowledge can inspire and persuade people to share their views and their knowledge.

Four Types of Companies Today

The potential for adding value is a crucial ingredient for success. We call this the knova (knowledge value) factor. It is determined by two factors: a company's knowledge intensity and the service level it provides. As shown in Figure 1, we have defined four broad categories of companies today: the industrial production company, the service-providing company, the knowledge-creating company, and the value-adding knowledge company.

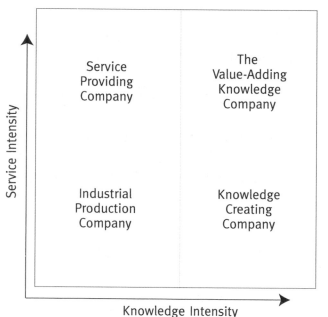

Figure 1. *The Knova Factor*

Source: R. Tissen, D. Andriessen, and F. Lekanne Deprez, *The Knowledge Dividend: Creating High-Performance Companies Through Value-Based Knowledge Management* (London: Financial Times/Prentice Hall, 2000), p. 9.

Industrial Production Companies

Examples of old-style industrial companies are getting increasingly difficult to find. Even producing a simple beer can require an enormous amount of knowledge.[2] So even production companies are having to get more knowledge-intensive.

Service-Providing Companies

A typical example of a service-providing company is an employment agency. These agencies originally emerged to satisfy the need of many companies for additional staff. It was often time consuming for companies to recruit temporary staff by themselves, so they avoided the hassle by turning to an agency. This was particularly true when staff was needed for only a limited period—to take over work from an employee on holiday or maternity leave, for example—and therefore could not be offered a full-time contract. However, contingent workers can be useful in a number of less traditional ways. Nowadays, there is part-time work, temporary employment, employee leasing, self-employment, insourcing, outsourcing, and home-based work. Virtually any work arrangement that might differ from the commonly perceived norm of full-time salaried job falls under the rubric of contingent work today. However, agencies do even more than provide these different types of workers. They have recognized that a high level of service is vital in what is becoming a highly competitive industry. How they supply staff has thus become more flexible; they may be offered for temporary work but also for longer periods on a contract or even for permanent employment.

The market for employment has become more transparent. It is easier for potential employers to reach potential employees than ever before. The Internet is proving particularly suitable for bringing together employer and employee. The agencies are under pressure; their traditional services are no longer enough to guarantee them future stability. So in order to continue adding value for their customers, they too have had to become more knowledge-intensive—that is, have a greater knowledge of both the candidates and the vacancies so a perfect match can be made. For this, increasingly sophisticated information systems are being used. In addition, many agencies are increasing the services they offer their clients by introducing training for the candidates, organizing seminars, and even establishing schools and academies for potential candidates.

Knowledge-Creating Companies and Value-Adding Knowledge Companies

I. Nonaka, H. Takeuchi, and K. Umemoto write: "Creating new knowledge is . . . not simply a matter of learning from others or acquiring knowledge from the outside. It has to build on its own, frequently requiring intensive and laborious interaction among members of the organization. . . . Western managers need to 'unlearn' their old mode of thinking that all knowledge is explicit and can be acquired and taught through manuals, books, or lectures."[3]

In their groundbreaking book *The Knowledge-Creating Company*, Nonaka and Takeuchi stress the importance of knowledge creation in modern companies.[4] But as the knova factor indicates, this is not enough. Companies are not in business to create knowledge but to add value. The knova factor shows that for a company to be successful in the emerging knowledge economy it will not be enough to concentrate on increasing either service levels or the knowledge intensity of its activities. Rather, both the level of service and the level of knowledge content need to increase to allow a company to move to greater success.

For many years, Amsterdam's Schiphol Airport has been nominated by international travelers as the best airport in the world. On the surface, the airport provides the same facilities as airports anywhere in the world: runways, terminals, service areas. Its success is the result of an ongoing determination to put the customer first. Management has the ability to see service and business through the customer's eyes. Attention has been given to matters such as signposting, space, light, convenient transfer support, train connections, and just plain fun. Passengers in the terminal can enjoy a wide range of facilities, including shops, offices, hotels, showers, restaurants, even a casino. The Schiphol Group, which manages the airport, knows how to create and exploit airport cities. It has successfully transferred its unique experience and expertise to other international airports, such as JFK in New York and Brisbane Airport in Australia. It is a value-adding knowledge company that not only services its customers best but exploits its unique knowledge and experience on a worldwide basis.

Owning Versus Sharing Knowledge

As knowledge becomes something that is shared, how can companies gain a strategic advantage, even for a short period of time, from the core knowledge they have at their disposal? When we break down the organizational barriers impeding the exchange of knowledge, we also destroy the barriers that protect our core knowledge from our competitors. Is there any way to maintain a strategic advantage when knowledge is freely available to everyone?

For a company to add value successfully, it needs access to knowledge that it can use to its own advantage. Already many companies are discovering that patents and copyrights are a profitable source of income. These intangible assets—once simply considered a means for production and protection—have become increasingly valuable because of the potential they offer companies to add value. But the protection of patents is short-lived and under pressure. Copying is just a click away and cannot be controlled.

Traditionally, many companies invested a considerable part of their income in fundamental research. In a closed industrial age environment, such investments were essential. Speed was not as important as technological in-house knowledge. Progress was made slowly, at a pace dictated by technology rather than by customers.

Today, that has changed. Markets lead. Successful companies anticipate or follow as swiftly as possible. Therefore, strategy and strategic thinking is "in" and not "out." Cor Boonstra, former CEO of Royal Philips Electronics in The Netherlands, was wrong: strategy does not equal market demand. It is no longer a question of supply and demand, but rather of demand and supply. Companies cannot wait for knowledge; they must have instant access to it. And they must have access to exactly that knowledge which they require at this specific moment. Not tomorrow, but now. Instantly. In zero time.

Thus, companies must not only have access to knowledge but actually own it, even if only for a short time—the time they need to get a head start on the competition.

To do this, they must adopt a policy of constant change. Acquisitions, joint ventures, knowledge alliances, and partnerships are no longer undertaken to expand a corporate empire but rather to acquire knowledge that complements existing in-house knowledge and can increase returns.

The drive to own knowledge, however, should never become an end in itself. A company's success is not measured in the amount of knowledge it owns but rather in the way it uses that knowledge to add value. Being able to use knowledge is far more important than being able to create knowledge. In fact, some of today's leading companies are witnessing a glut of knowledge. Jennifer Brown, vice president of Fidelity Investments, an e-business company, confesses that the company has more good ideas than it can handle. "We have so many good ideas here—truly innovative ideas—that sometimes our people get a little frustrated that we can't act on more of them," she says.[5] Nor is this situation confined to smaller operations; e-commerce innovators—think of eBay, Amazon.com, Microsoft—all generate more ideas than they are capable of using.

Creating knowledge and owning knowledge must become secondary to using knowledge to add value. A successful company will own assets, and know how to make the most of them.

But there is another side to all this: the assets a company owns determine its strength in a competitive marketplace. A company that owns assets becomes an attractive partner in an alliance. When knowledge is up for grabs, the strongest party will win the prize.

All this implies a totally new way of conducting business. The focus of a company's business must shift constantly. Everything must become more pragmatic—here today, gone tomorrow. It will become increasingly restrictive to harness oneself into a single business, even if it is based on a core competence that has been carefully nurtured for many years. A core competence must be seen as an enabler rather than a definer. Sony, for example, is no longer an audio equipment manufacturer but rather an entertainment provider.

REINVENTING SONY: HOW THE PLAYSTATION BECAME SONY'S TICKET TO THE DIGITAL AGE

Ken Kutaragi, an obscure Sony researcher, got his company to join the digital economy almost single-handedly. The PlayStation is the only Sony product that the company can point to as a pure example of software-hardware synergy. The problem, as Kutaragi saw it, was that Sony's historical strengths lay with analog technologies, the sort found in televisions, VCRs, and tape players. Meanwhile, the company was behind in three of the hot new digital markets: personal computers, cell phones, and videogames. Kutaragi lobbied senior management tirelessly: 'I convinced them that computer entertainment would be very important in the future. Sony had established itself as an analog provider, but it had to convert itself into a digital, information-based company in the future. No one realized that.'

"Kutaragi threatened to leave the company if he wasn't allowed to proceed with his video game project. And he made an outrageous promise: if the company would fund his R&D efforts, he would create a platform for Sony's future growth. Kutaragi kept his promise. Launched in Japan during Christmas 1994, the PlayStation was the first thirty-two-bit game machine on the market. As sales shot skyward, Sony Computer Entertainment (the group that developed the PlayStation) was awarded divisional status inside Sony. In 1999 Kutaragi, the onetime outcast, became CEO of the division. By the end of fiscal year 1999, Sony had sold 55 million PlayStations worldwide and 430 million copies of videogame software. Sony Computer Entertainment racked up $6.5 billion in revenues, with a mouthwatering 17 percent operating margin, compared with 5 percent for the company as a whole. It was the company's second largest business, ahead of music and movies, trailing only Sony Electronics."[6]

In sum, a company that defines itself in products rather than customer requirements is doomed to fail. A company whose core competence is manufacturing doors is less likely to succeed than a competitor that sees its competence as "entrance technology."

In other words, what a company does is less important than what it *can* do. This means leaving options open. It means being able to move through uncharted territory until a signpost looms up in the fog, and then changing direction instantly—and profitably.

As companies move from one alliance or partnership to another, what they do becomes less important than what they know. Cutting-edge companies no longer develop knowledge in order to manufacture a product; rather, they innovate in order to make themselves attractive to potential partners.

With more attention being placed on co-ownership, comakership, and codevelopment, suppliers are no longer being told what to produce but rather what customer problem to solve. As product life cycles grow shorter, solving new problems becomes more important than supplying products. Manufacturing—the very heart of successful industrial age companies—is now little more than an afterthought. In fact, it has transformed itself into what we might call *mind*facturing. Even the great industrial giants are realizing that it is no longer necessary, or even advisable, to do everything in-house. Outsourcing to specialized contractors—companies that own specialized knowledge—provides a degree of flexibility that is of far greater value in a market where customer satisfaction is the most important thing. The traditional "not invented here" mentality must be replaced with "proudly invented elsewhere."

Employee share ownership plans can help increase the company's eventual success in business by inspiring everyone to think and act like owners.[7]

Intangible assets are the new commodities. Which intangible assets do you need at this specific moment in your company portfolio? Where do you find them? Which partner can offer you the greatest complementary benefits? It is no longer a question of knowing something but of knowing where to find—where to acquire—something. Just as a financial investor constantly shifts his interests from one stock to another, so a zero space company will acquire and sell its intangible stock. Ongoing reevaluation of how best to meet changing customer demands will no longer be seen as a sign of indecision but rather as an indication of strength.

Go Forth and Multiply

Sharing knowledge means increasing knowledge, but many people have difficulty in verbalizing or writing down what they know. A zero space company will never share indiscriminately. Instead, it will share to increase the effectiveness and competitiveness of the knowledge it will acquire in return. And it will know what *not* to share. It will understand which knowledge is needed to allow things to multiply.

It is all about acquiring complementary knowledge. This is totally different from the traditional strategy of acquiring more of the same, building up gigantic monoliths to showcase success to the outside world.

Successful companies will not construct vast cities; instead they will become the nomads of industry. They will be hard to target because they have little physical infrastructure to focus on. They will move unfettered from place to place, drinking at one oasis one day and another the next. They will stay on the alert for the next signpost. They will see, move, arrive, do business, and then move on.

The challenge for managers is enormous. It is much easier and more comfortable to concentrate on the well-known than to remain on the lookout for the unknown. But in zero space, there is no final destination; moving along the road is everything.

How often have we used the phrase *a meeting of great minds*? But how often do we think of applying it to business? Traditionally, companies aimed for mergers, for acquisitions. The need to own, to embrace, to grow bigger was behind many such moves. "If you can't beat them—buy them" seemed to be the battle cry. Of course, tangible assets can be combined— by integrating production facilities, centralizing manufacturing, streamlining logistics—but how do you combine intangible assets? Frankenstein experiments—transferring brains into bodies—are as frighteningly impossible today as they were in Mary Shelley's time.

A meeting of great minds. Find a companion with whom you can walk a short distance, exchange ideas, share experiences. And then part company and move on in other directions. This is the way companies operate in zero space.

The Manager's Changing Role

How can a manager plot a path through uncharted territory? Is it possible to set a course and then follow it blindly? Of course not. Yet the traditional role of the manager is to control, to coordinate, to manage.

But this is not the role of the manager in the knowledge-based economy. Today managers must be directors, conductors. They must orchestrate activities so that teamwork results in adding value. Managers no longer work in banking, marketing, manufacturing, IT, or advertising, but rather *between* these areas.

Certainly with the changing role of professionals—and their desire to move freely from one challenging position to the next—it is vital that individual qualities be harnessed into a coherent performance. Reprising the jazz analogy introduced earlier, business is becoming similar to jazz, where session players meet, make music together, and then move on to play with other professionals. The director—or leader of the band—must understand which forces are required at any given moment, and must know where to find them. It is no good hiring a bass player to play a trombone score.

No live performance is ever perfect. That is not the way of the world. Yet an exhilarating performance, one that captures the imagination, depends on the ability to commit to a team for the moment. The band leader must possess the "quiet drive" to let others shine, inspire the band to work together, and give their best. But ultimately, the music is made by the band.

THE IMPROVISING ORGANIZATION

"Examining different groups of musicians, and contrasting those practicing in a symphony to those practicing in a jazz quartet, yields the following insight. The coordinating and integrating mechanisms in a symphony orchestra are the musical score and the conductor. These musicians operate in a professional capacity, meaning, for most individuals, they don't have to like one another. By contrast, jazz improvisation requires a high degree of trust and mutual respect; these musicians self-integrate and are often good friends."[8]

In zero space, managers must be able to direct the whole chain of activities. They must be able to think in processes, to ensure that each process meshes seamlessly with the next. They must be able to concentrate on directing all the processes, and then leave the execution to the team. They have to co-sense and co-create the future.[9]

Hands-on management is not possible when you are dealing with intangibles. Hands-off direction is the new management creed—at least for those hoping to succeed in zero space.

PART II

The Eight Key Features of Zero Space

3

Zero Space— Infinite Potential

O RGANIZATIONS ARE FLUID AFFAIRS, reflecting the changing needs of business and society. Ideally, they are flexible and reactive; unfortunately, in reality they are often cast in stone. But as we move further into the knowledge-based economy, any old ideas that we may have held about organizations must be cast aside.

The idea of companies as fluid entities is not new. As long ago as 1972, M. D. Cohen, J. G. March, and J. P. Olson introduced the so-called garbage can model into organizational science.[1] What this suggested is that organizational space is nothing more than a mixture of people, solutions, choices, and problems that simply float round aimlessly until they happen to coincide and create a solution. This was a cynical commentary on the organizations of the old economy but there was much truth in the observation. Many companies spent increasing amounts of time trying to organize the garbage can.

Today, things are different. As we already discussed in Part I, the invisible, the intangible, is now what counts.

Traditional organizations, with their clear lines of authority and structure provided a framework. There was a place for everybody, and all knew their place. But as the boundaries become increasingly vague, people working in organizations become anxious. Friction and conflict increase. Paralysis may result. An organization without boundaries can seem intimidating. Nevertheless, it is essential to recognize that the old boundaries are restrictive and need to be broken down.

FOUR TYPES OF BOUNDARIES IN ORGANIZATIONS

There are many boundaries in present-day organizations and cultures. In fact, four types of boundaries have been defined:[2]

- *Vertical* boundaries exist between levels and ranks of people.
- *Horizontal* boundaries exist between functions and disciplines.
- *External* boundaries exist between the organization and its suppliers, customers, and regulators.
- *Geographic* boundaries exist between cultures and markets.

Figure 2 shows the eight areas of a zero space organization. It is essential to focus on all eight key features in order to create an organization that is flexible and fluid but also stable and enduring.

On the surface, these two criteria may seem contradictory. How can something be both flexible and stable, fluid and enduring?

To answer those questions, we have to take another look at the current state of affairs. We have come to equate *organization* with something that fills space, something that exists physically, a tangible expression of success. Office buildings, headquarters, factories, nameplates on doors, heavy conference tables, impressive offices, little boxes on charts—in a world that thinks in a material way all these things remain the epitome of enduring fame and fortune. But do any of these things matter in the new knowledge-based economy? Are opulent offices essential in an economy where more and more people work on-line? Are organizations ruled by functional thinking relevant in an economy where processes are everything?

In zero space we create something that exists now and has the ability and the flexibility to exist into the future and to adapt to that future, whatever it may be. The last thing we want is a here-today-and-gone-tomorrow organization. An organization in the knowledge-based economy will become snakelike: ready to shed its skin when it has outlived its usefulness.

The next chapters take a closer look at the eight key features of zero space.

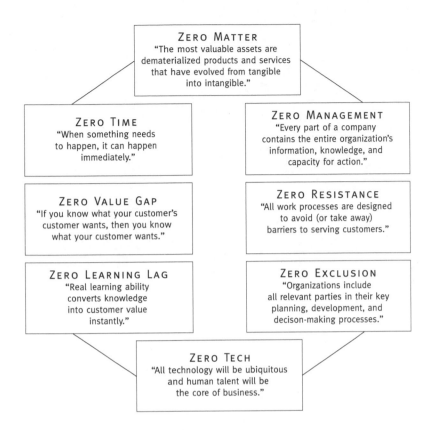

Figure 2. *Zero Space Organizations*

Source: Inspired by R. Yeh, K. Pearson, and G. Kozmetsky, *Zero Time* (New York: Wiley, 2000).

4

ZERO MATTER

▪ ▪ ▪ ▪ ▪ ▪ ▪ ▪ ▪ ▪ ▪ ▪ ▪ ▪

M ATTER USED TO RULE THE WORLD, but it doesn't any longer. We may have lived in a material world once, but now we live in a world that is virtually matter-less. In fact, the less matter you have, the better. As G. Wolf wrote: "The fewer atoms you move, the more money you make."[1]

In the old economy, tangible assets were at the heart of a financially solid company. But in the knowledge-based economy, intangibles are the key to success—intangibles and the market's perception of the company's potential. For today the value of a company is increasingly determined by market traders rather than accountants.

At no time has the gap between book value and market value been so great. Yet this is not surprising. Book value concentrates on historical data, whereas market value concentrates on a company's potential to generate profit. In their book *Weightless Wealth* Daniel Andriessen and René Tissen wrote: "Financial reporting systems reveal little of the assets which today, in the knowledge economy, play a vital role in the success (and continued success) of the company. Nor do present financial indicators give any true picture of the key factors for success. And a balance sheet says very little about future success."[2]

The enormous explosion of interest in companies that are low in substance and high in promise may seem a recent phenomenon, but the trend away from tangible assets toward intangible assets was under way for much of the twentieth century. In 1929 the ratio of intangible business capital to tangible business capital was 30:70; by 1990 that had changed to 63:37.[3]

Nevertheless, nothing, it has to be admitted, could have prepared the world for the way in which the money market now rules the actual market. A company with no means of making money—at least in the traditional way of thinking—until very recently could find its stock rocketing through the ceiling with the market valuing the company very highly indeed. In fact, we seemed to be moving into an era in which financial hype was the one determining factor for the value of a company. And nothing else—particularly not matter—mattered.

This new system has a downside, of course, as demonstrated by the sudden demise of many NASDAQ companies. These companies' stock, once so highly regarded, suddenly plummeted in value, as if the market and investors had decided en masse that their initial enthusiasm was misplaced.

What Has Amazon.com Learned from the Dot-Com Crash?

According to Jeffrey Bezos, CEO of Amazon.com: "We have learned that *the company is not the stock*. The clearest way I can describe it is that back in the year 1999, when the stock market was booming and Amazon stock prices were booming, we had about fourteen million customers buying from us. In 2000, when the stock was busting, we had about twenty million customers buying from us. So if the stock is the company, somebody forgot to tell the customers."[4]

Perhaps this was little more than an adjustment in market thinking as investors began to question the earning capacity of many dot-com companies. Indeed, the demise of some of the cutting-edge leaders in that sector allowed the rest of us to realize their true value. Professor William Sahlman of Harvard Business School believes that it is important to separate the value of the business created by the new economy from its stock prices: "Amazon.com, for example, opens up a whole bunch of purchasing possibilities for consumers. I can shop at midnight. It's also a compelling business model. I pay up-front, but they don't pay their suppliers for sixty days. Having said that, was Amazon worth $40 billion? No, it wasn't. But that doesn't change the fact that Amazon still represents $4 or $5 billion worth of value that was created by a real transformation."[5]

Valuing Intangible Assets

One of today's most pressing needs is a reliable accounting method for a zero matter environment, one in which the emphasis shifts from tangible assets to intangible ones. In *Weightless Wealth* Andriessen and Tissen propose a radical new method for assessing the value that intangible assets contribute to a company's strategic future. Although it allows managers to put a financial value on their company's intangibles, its main power is to give managers a tool with which to calculate the value-adding potential of existing intangibles in combination with the company's core competencies.[6]

All too often, a company gets bogged down in its own business. Managers seem to think that a traditional core competence will remain at the heart of its business, no matter what. Yet core competencies—just like markets—can erode and decline. It is important to assess the sustainability of a core competence and to calculate the contribution it makes to the business not only today but also in the future.

Andriessen and Tissen's method allows managers to examine the value of core competencies *over time*. A core competence that makes an important contribution to a company's profits today (and it is the contribution to profits that is the key issue here) may not make the same contribution tomorrow. On the other hand, one that seems of secondary importance today may prove to be the cash cow of tomorrow. By allowing managers to calculate the changing value a competence brings to the company's results, the authors provide them with a strategic tool for defining their acquisition, investment, and strategic priorities.

The authors define five types of intangible assets, as shown in Figure 3.

- *Skills and tacit knowledge* are the talents of the people in the company, including their competencies and know-how.
- *Collective values and norms* make up the corporate culture of an organization. They are reflected in "the way we do things around here." They describe what the organization feels to be important (client focus, reliability, quality, and so on) and are often a crucial factor in its success.

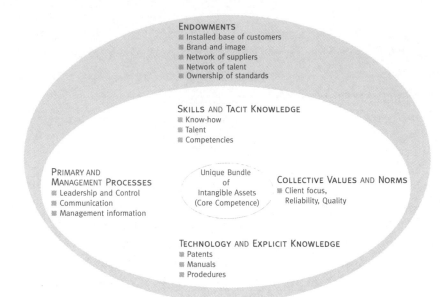

Figure 3. *A Core Competence as a Unique Bundle of Intangible Assets*

Source: D. Andriessen, "Weightless Wealth: Four Modifications to Standard IC Theory," *Journal of Intellectual Capital* 2(3) 2001, p. 211.

- *Technology and explicit knowledge* include manuals, procedures, and intellectual property, such as patents and trade secrets.
- *Primary and management processes* are the knowledge embedded in the primary processes of the organization, plus the processes that are used for management.
- *Endowments* are what a company has inherited from the past, including brand and image, networks of suppliers, installed base of customers, network of talent, and ownership of standards.

In order to identify the interrelationships between intangible assets that are important strategically, the figure shows a link with the company's core competencies. According to G. Hamel and C. K. Prahalad's theory of core competencies, the real future of a company lies in neither the products or services it provides nor in its market share but rather in the optimal use and maintenance of its unique skills—that is, its core competencies. This concept has become important because it allows companies to define themselves, their markets, and their added value in a new way, leading to many new and often unexpected opportunities.[7]

Close analysis of core competencies shows that they almost always consist of a combination of intangible assets—knowledge and skills—that flourish in a particular culture. Although tangible assets also play a role in core competencies, they are often buildings, such as a global network of sales offices. Such property makes a contribution to the core competencies but does not constitute an essential part of them.

So the analysis of intangible assets begins by defining the company's core competencies. Generally, a company will have between five and ten of them. The company will have made an inventory of its most important intangible assets. This can be used as a basis to structure the intellectual capital (IC) report. An IC report describes the paramount importance of human capital (the company's know-how, including the collective experience and skills, which is not owned by the company) and structured capital (the company's supporting resources and infrastructure, including all the assets found in its financial statement). It then becomes clear what the impact on the realization of the company's strategy is if the share of employees with advanced degrees who contribute to a specific core competence goes up.

Andriessen and Tissen then drew up a list of criteria to help determine the practical strength of each bundle of intangible assets, that is, each core competence. Each core competence has five criteria, as follows:

It Adds Value for Customers

Does the core competence being analyzed create a substantial benefit for customers or provide the company with a substantial cost benefit? This is a vital point, because we are now entering the knowledge-based economy, where, author Kevin Kelly writes, companies need to add more value at less cost.[8] Hamel and Prahalad, in their book *Competing for the Future*, call the concept *customer value*.

It Provides a Competitive Edge

Is the company better in this specific competence than its competitors? Does this competence make it unique? As we have already seen, a competence that is shared by every company in an industry is little more than a skill, unless one company is significantly better at it than the others. Hamel and Prahalad call this *competitor differentiation.*

It Offers Potential for the Future

The life cycle of products is decreasing all the time. Only a decade ago, the life cycle of a PC was calculated in years, now it is frequently calculated in months. This means that companies must get their products to market faster than ever before. As British comedian John Cleese put it recently: "We've spent the last thirty years developing an incredible number of labor-saving appliances—and the result is we have less time than ever before." In business, we are, quite simply, living in a time when there is never enough time! Core competencies must be able to feed innovation, so that a company can beat competitors to the marketplace. They must provide the gateway to the markets of tomorrow. Hamel and Prahalad call this *extendability.*

It Is Sustainable for Several Years

Will the quality of the competence stay ahead of the competition for a substantial period of time? Or will it be something that the competition will be able to pick up simply, thus destroying the advantage?

It Is Firmly Anchored in the Organization

A competence that is shared by just a tiny group of individuals is of little use; these people may leave and take the competence with them. This was brought home very clearly to ING Barings Bank, when half of its very successful Taiwanese team, which had achieved record trading on the growing Taiwanese stock exchange, defected to Merrill Lynch. A core competence must be rooted in the organization, shared by most of the people in it. But we should issue a word of warning here: beware of core rigidities. "We've always done it that way" should not mean "That is the only way we are prepared to do it."

To help managers test their intangible assets, Andriessen and Tissen developed a checklist for each of the five criteria. Each one provides a series of questions to ask when judging the competencies. (The full check-list can be downloaded from the Web at www.weightlesswealth.com.) The result of applying these tests is then used as input to create a strategic management agenda. This agenda will be the guide for strategic decisions about the health of their intangible assets.

Benefiting from Knowledge

As companies move into zero space they must realize that owning assets is no longer a guarantee of success. Instead, they must learn new ways to benefit from assets that do not need to be in their exclusive possession. Knowledge—the driver of the present economy—cannot be encapsulated in buildings or tangible assets; it is in the minds of people. Only by finding ways to encourage people to recombine knowledge into new products and services can companies gain a competitive advantage.

But there is another side to zero matter: knowledge on its own is not enough. Knowledge only becomes powerful when it is put to work. All too often, companies fall into the trap of assuming that knowing about something is all that they need to do. They "know" about e-commerce, they "know" about networks, they "know" about intangibles. Knowledge is power, they think. And it is. But knowledge is the power *to do*. Unless that knowledge is turned into action, companies become eunuchs in the business harem: they know what to do, they've seen it done a thousand times, but they can't do it themselves!

The strength of a knowledge-driven company is not in its constant acquisition of more of the same but rather in its ability to combine existing knowledge—whether it is in-house or possessed by a strategic partner—into new products and services that are likely to create value for the company. The value field must be carefully surveyed, charted, and then navigated to ensure that the company is moving toward increased profits.

Only when it is understood that knowledge is never an end in itself but simply a means to an end, will companies take a big step into zero space. Then they must understand that success depends on a constant, continuous process of combining and recombining knowledge into something new. Something that customers—and the customer's customers—really want.

This process has several stages, as illustrated in the knowledge pyramid shown in Figure 4.

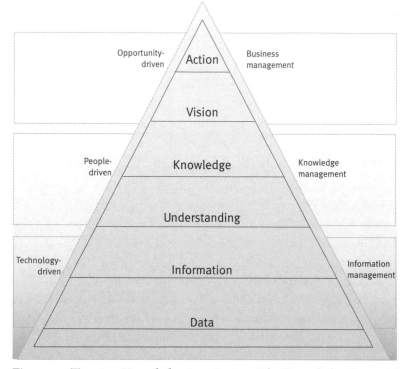

Figure 4. *Turning Knowledge into Action: The Knowledge Pyramid*
Source: KPMG Knowledge Advisory Services, 2001.

The base of any knowledge structure is *data*. It is vital that a data-gathering and storing system is established in the company. The system must allow not only ease of input but also ease of access. Everybody in a knowledge-rich company must understand the importance of input, the importance of data. But they mustn't allow themselves the illusion that that is where everything comes to an end. It is only the start.

Data as such are worth nothing. For example, knowing the word *Washington* doesn't provide any clues about the city itself. It is just data. It is only when you start combining it with other pieces of data that you start getting *information*. *Washington, D.C.* combined with the *White House* combined with the *Lincoln Memorial* provides information. But it remains merely information to anyone who has not visited Washington; it becomes *understanding* when the city is actually included in a travel itinerary. Still even that remains superficial. No one who visits Washington once can claim to have *knowledge* of it. For that, you really need to share your information with someone who has lived or worked there for many years. This, ultimately, can lead to *action*—to discovering the heartbeat of the city.

In business, we have to take the same path. Data need to be combined to provide information. And we then have to understand that information. Only when we share our understanding—create a shared *vision*—can we move to action.

The challenge is to move swiftly through these stages, to create a zero matter, zero time organization in which this path can be negotiated as swiftly and as painlessly as possible.

In today's zero space organization, zero matter is a serious business. It is much easier to negotiate an obstacle course—one that is pitted with danger, with competitors trying to take the lead—if you are not weighed down with unnecessary assets.

5

ZERO TIME

■ ■ ■ ■ ■ ■ ■ ■ ■ ■

WE LIVE IN A TIME in which there is never enough time. As the speed of business accelerates, we are becoming a click-and-go society. Impatience, instead of the exception, is now the norm. We no longer have the time—or the inclination—to wait. A recent management book encapsulated the customer expectations in the title: *Free, Perfect, and Now.*[1]

Operating in Net Time

The impact of the Internet cannot be underestimated in the changing attitudes about time in business. With a click we can travel around the world, gaining instant access to information and items for sale. We order an item and then wait for weeks for it to arrive. There is a time lag between our expectations and the ability of the company to deliver.

A company that can deliver faster than its competitors enjoys a competitive edge. This need to move faster is highlighted by a war currently taking place between two Dutch mail-order companies. In a new offensive, the number two company is committed to delivering any ordered item within twenty-four hours.

THE TIME IS THE PRESENT, THE DISTANCE IS ZERO

According to T. A. Stewart, "Whatever a customer wants, he wants it now. Present time is what I have to deliver."[2] Real time is what you have to manage. A customer might not want your service all the time, but she might want it at any time; therefore you have to be ready all the time.

Speed of action is paralleled by speed of growth. Raymond Yeh says: "It used to take twenty years to become a $1 billion company. Now it takes as little as three years."[3] In fact, in some cases success is no longer judged by the turnover but rather by the speed with which that turnover is achieved. According to some commentators, we are about to witness a massive disturbance. To quote Lou Gerstner, chairman and CEO of IBM, "The real story that's arriving is when thousands and thousands of institutions that exist today seize the power of this global computing and communications infrastructure and use it to transform themselves. That's the real revolution."[4]

The dot-com coup d'état introduced a new term into the business vocabulary: *Net time*. In *Culture.com*, this concept is explained in some detail:

> It is generally assumed that Net time is a ten to one ratio, meaning that business is transacted ten times faster than it was traditionally (even a few years ago). This means that changes that once took ten years to happen are now taking place in one year. Chase Manhattan launched its new company "ChaseShop" in partnership with ShopNow.com and took only eighteen weeks to get all its lines of business to sign off on the new infrastructure and have the Web site designed, tested, and rolled out. Mike Mazza, vice president of Chase's Internet project office said: "Traditionally in a large corporation, in eighteen weeks you can't even have two meetings."[5]

The need for zero time is reinforced by the speed of innovation. Life cycles are becoming increasingly brief. Obsolescence is built into much more than just fashion. Research and development are constantly battling against this ongoing pressure to perform faster. Eric Schmidt, chief technology officer at Sun Microsystems, talks of "Web weeks" in R&D. He estimates that 20 percent of the knowledge generated in his company is obsolete within a year.[6] Theo Classen, chief technology officer at Philips Semiconductors, maintains that technology suppliers are no longer judged only on the quality and reliability of their products but also on the speed with which those products can be developed and brought to market. [7]

Nor is this acceleration limited to professional products. Even in the world of consumer goods, speed is becoming essential. As tastes change and develop, companies must be alert to new directions in the market and react efficiently and effectively. Any other course of action would result in a lag that could mean corporate death.

This is also true in those markets that are traditionally based on customer loyalty—the beer market, for example. Beer drinkers tend to remain loyal to a specific brand, perhaps because only a limited number of brands are available. But the beer market is as sensitive to change as any other. The Miller Brewing Company provides a good illustration. In the early 1990s, 90 percent of its revenue came from beers that had not existed two years earlier.[8]

The Cash Flow Lag

One of the biggest problems for many companies is cash flow. The lapse in time between financing operations and receiving payment can often cause a serious money shortage. Stock reduction and just-in-time (JIT) operations were designed to free up the capital that many companies had invested in tangible assets. Many automobile companies are moving toward mass-customization in order to ensure that only those cars that are ordered actually get manufactured. Logistics in supermarket operations are becoming a core competence; instant adjustment of stock in response to customer buying behaviors is now an essential part of the operation. The networking of stock control, linking all orders to actual purchases, allows such operations to be more customer-focused and less vulnerable to projections.

Many leading companies in consumer goods are taking all this one step further and starting to operate in *negative* time. Here, income is generated *before* a product is manufactured. Dell Computers, for example, expects its customers to pay with a credit card when they place their order. Thus the money is already in the bank before even the first screw is fitted. This also means that Dell is able to pay its suppliers *after* it has received its income. The result is a cash conversion cycle of a *negative* eight days!

Speeded-Up Consumer Demand

The speed of change is so hectic that there is little time for adjustment. For example, the growth in the use of cell telephones has been staggering. In 1998 there were 250 million cell phones worldwide; by the year 2000 that number had soared to 600 million! To put this growth into better perspective, consider this. It took well over half a century for the telephone to reach a high level of penetration. Today, the same penetration rate for cell phones has been reached in a mere half-decade. The industry is now producing on the order of 200 million units each year; in fact, more cell phones are now being produced worldwide than either cars or televisions.[9]

Much of the growth is generated by the astounding array of services that are constantly being developed and offered to consumers. The cell phone industry is working at a rate similar to the fashion industry, offering a new collection every three months. New services are introduced almost weekly, from short messaging service (SMS) to wireless application protocol (WAP). And customers are eager to make use of them. In fact, consumers now replace their cell telephones once every ten months. All this in a market that is only a decade old.

But there are literally thousands of new products fighting for the consumer's attention. And so the rate of success is paralleled by the rate of failure. The window of opportunity is narrowing. It is no longer measured in years but in weeks. Too late is worse than never. People now realize that it is not labor, capital, information, or innovation that is in short supply but rather human attention. We are, as we have already said, living in a time when there is never enough time. The tortoise and the hare? Slow and steady wins the race? Not in today's zero time economy!

A question that is now being asked is whether, in this age of instant obsolescence, the concept of ownership has any meaning. Will consumers be prepared to invest in a product that may be out of date before they get it home? Jonathan Wright and Jeremy Rifkin see car ownership as a thing of the past: "Today, one-third of the cars and trucks in the United States are leased. Twenty years from now in the United States, Europe, Asia, and Latin America, no one's going to own a car except as an oddity. If Ford had its way, it would rather never sell another car again."[10]

Never sell another car again? Certainly, because that's the difference between a market economy and a network economy. Understanding the importance of customer loyalty—one of those intangibles that are constantly mentioned in the knowledge-based economy—means ensuring that a constant dialogue is maintained with the customer. This cannot be guaranteed in a simple buy-sell relationship. That is a one-off, single-moment-in-time event. It does not lead to an ongoing relationship. As Wright and Rifkin put it: "[Ford] would much rather that you and I paid for the experience of driving than for the vehicle."[11]

Speeded-Up Business Relationships

If customer relationships are changing, so too are business partnerships. Alliances and partnerships are no longer cast in stone; they are fluid, adapting to the changing needs of the market. This morning's competitor becomes this afternoon's partner. And Internet partnerships—that is, any alliance formed around an e-business strategy—are much faster, more agile, and more likely to satisfy the changing needs of the customer. It is a "match-and-go" relationship that mirrors the "click-and-go" environment of the Internet: a temporary alliance—during which the partners offer value to each other—which is disbanded when no longer necessary, often in as little as six months.

Such an attitude, in a world where acquisitions, takeovers, and mergers are seen as a sign of strength—"My company is bigger than your company"—not only is foreign but goes against the grain of everything that traditional managers believe. Impermanence is the last thing they want, yet it is becoming the first thing they need. Zero time implies a new manner of operating. It is not just about moving faster, beating the competition over the line. It isn't just about finding ways of keeping ever-shorter cycle times and product life cycles under control. It isn't just about doing the same old things you've always done, but also about doing them quicker.

Zero time implies a simple attitude: think and act almost in one continuous process. It means recognizing a need and immediately satisfying it. "In the new digital competition, just being faster is not enough," write Yeh, Pearson, and Kozmetsky.[12] "To win, we must see differently and act instantly. We must operate in zero time." And to do that we must learn to respond instantaneously to a new customer need. Without endless meetings or time-consuming studies. *We see, therefore we act.* A new credo? Perhaps. But certainly a total break from the past when everything was planned and controlled, and customers were prepared to wait for companies to come up with something resembling what they wanted.

Still, in today's mad-dash society, not everybody can keep up all the time. In many companies there are people who simply cannot keep pace with Net time innovations. Managers must recognize this. They must understand that in such a driven economy it is sometimes prudent to slow down a little. And this is particularly true when attracting, retaining, and inspiring human capital. As Marcus Buckingham and Curt Coffman commented: "People leave managers—not companies."[13]

Zero time is more than simply acting faster. It is not about the speed of reaction; instead it is about the speed of anticipation. For many companies, this means moving into negative time. As the market moves with the speed of fright, it is no longer sufficient to wait until something happens and then move to capitalize on it. If a company is unable to anticipate its customers' needs and hopes to remain successful by reacting to them by offering me-too products, then its chance for sustainable growth is nil.

Strategizing in Zero Time

The big question is where all this leaves strategy. Certainly traditional strategic tools such as alternative scenarios and long-term market analyses fit in poorly with zero time thinking. Five-year plans have little to contribute to a market that can change radically overnight.

Today, any inflexible strategy will only prove disastrous. As knowledge combines, a fast change of course is essential. Companies that continue like mammoth oil tankers—that change course in days rather than seconds—will inevitably shipwreck on the unseen rocks of competition. A compass and a chart are leftovers from less stressful voyages.

In any rapidly changing landscape, a detailed itinerary is of little use. Instead, you need to plan the general direction of your journey and then allow yourself to explore the roads that present themselves. A strategic journey becomes an exploration. The spirit of Columbus reigns. We must allow ourselves to stumble over success. We must learn to travel through uncharted territory as if we had lived in such a landscape all our lives.

There is a Buddhist saying: *There is no road to happiness; happiness is the road.* In today's rapidly changing circumstances, we can rephrase that this way: *There is no road to success; success is the road.* Any strategy that focuses on some far-off goal is doomed to fail. Strategy must focus instead on the journey—and allow us to change direction instantly.

6

ZERO VALUE GAP

H OW OFTEN DO products and services disappoint because they do not meet the customer's expectations? How big is the gap between promise and result, expectation and reality? Is there a difference between what a customer wants and what a company thinks that customer wants?

The Dangerous Value Gap

This has always been a great concern for all manufacturers and service providers. But in a time when the window of opportunity has become so small, it becomes more crucial than ever. You only have one opportunity—and if you get it wrong, you won't get another shot at it.

Any value gap threatens the very existence of a company. This is why so many companies invest enormously in getting to know their customers and understanding them. The true value of customers as a major competitive asset is gradually seeping through to all layers of business.

But customer satisfaction—as important as that is—only comes into its own when it leads to customer share. Yeh, Pearson, and Kozmetsky define this as the volume of business a customer does with a certain company versus its competitors over the course of the customer's lifetime.[1] In other words, a company must determine the extent of a customer's loyalty and how it can take steps to ensure that loyalty over time.

How can a company do that? According to Yeh, Pearson, and Kozmetsky: "If you know what your customer's customer wants, then you know what your customer wants."[2] It is a question of projecting your thoughts always further down the industrial value chain.

FROM VALUE CHAIN TO VALUE FIELD: BASELL EXPERIENCES THE END OF THE (INDUSTRIAL) CHAIN AS WE KNOW IT

Managers in global companies are used to focusing on a fairly predictable flow of processes that are controlled and coordinated from inside the company. Nowadays, organizations must keep track of multiple relationships to deal with a variety of partners, alliances, or (on-line) customers. In a networked world, where everyone and everything is linked, the value chain metaphor is inadequate. Rather than being centralized in discrete units, a company's competencies are becoming "distributed." The IT infrastructure (portals, intranet, Internet) lets geographically dispersed individuals, teams, and communities connect to serve customers.

Breaking the links of the value chain does not mean neglecting the issues of gaining internal efficiencies or "undermanaging" operations or distribution.[3,4] These capabilities matter more than ever, but they can be considered a minimal license to operate and will not provide a sustainable competitive advantage. Basell, a global polyolefin company with customers in more than 120 countries and operations in 26 countries across five continents, dealt with clients and suppliers according to the traditional value chain. But with the increase of on-line, Web-enabled links with suppliers and clients, Basell has organized itself as a constellation of customers and suppliers that are engaged in a rich web of relationships. In a value constellation, the focus moves from activities performed by enterprises to a reconfiguration of roles and relationships among a constellation of suppliers, business partners, and customers so as to mobilize the creation of value in new forms by new players.[5] Kees Linse, COO of Basell NV, has experienced the transformation of a traditional linear value chain into a *value field* in his company and he describes it as follows:

"Whereas in the traditional value chain you had the customer and the customer's customer, we now have multiple relationships, which include both—for example, a car manufacturer that buys molded products from a molder but buys the raw plastic from us, or at least includes the commercial terms of the plastic supply in its overall assessment of its sourcing of molded products. Obviously, we have at the same time a relationship with the molder, whom we supply with raw material and whose performance in the plant is critically dependent on the attributes of the plastic we supply. However, these attributes for the molder are not the same as the ones that the car manufacturer values—he looks at the quality of the final product, what is made—the molder looks at the manufacturing process—how it is made. Therefore, there is not a single value chain, but rather a value field.

"This field is even larger than the example suggests. If you ever get the chance to go to the plastics fair in Dusseldorf, Germany, you will understand what I mean. There are large halls with raw materials producers, and with molders, but the value field becomes visible when you see that there are additive producers, pigment producers, machine producers, recyclers, and so on. You cannot avoid speaking almost of a "value channel" where at any stage a number of players are intimately depending on each other, but, and this is absolutely essential, via different attributes of the same product.

"The essential point is that more than one of the players may be interfacing with you at the same time while they are also interfacing with each other. And that is what creates a value field rather than a value chain."

Understanding the Real Customer

As we move through a world that is constantly shifting, where demands change and partners change, where products become obsolete as soon as they hit the streets, it is no longer sufficient to take a narrow view of customers and their needs. It is impossible to say with any certainty, "This is my customer." Tomorrow, that customer may become your supplier. Or your supplier's supplier. We now live in a business environment in which things don't remain the same for more than five minutes. But if you approach this problem zero-mindedly, you have a better chance of being able to adapt to the new situation so that you can achieve a zero value gap.

The well-known French scientist and consultant Claude Fussler said what most companies are now starting to do is to make their clients dependent on the manner in which they serve them: "The success of a company depends on the manner in which we service our customers. For the continuation of this success, we must know what our customers will want in five or ten years. The question is, how do we determine a demand which at present doesn't seem likely, when our customers are still satisfied, we make a profit, and we have a stable company?"[6] Fussler wrote this in 1997, yet the speed of change has already surpassed much of what he wrote. Knowing what customers will want in five or ten years has now become knowing what customers will want in five or ten months. In some industries, it has even become knowing what they will want in five or ten weeks. However, the essence of the thought remains valid: we must learn to understand the needs of customers—and our customers' customers.

Zero value gap means breaking out of the vicious cycle of playing catch-up with customers' needs. That is a soul-destroying process for any company—constantly realizing that it is one step behind the needs of its customers. It has led to reengineering, reorganization, and often refinancing. It forces a company to introduce new products, new services, and new processes, all designed to meet the expressed needs of customers, only to find that when they actually appear, the customers' taste and desires have changed—and the company is left holding the bag.

When does a company actually suffer from a value gap? Yeh, Pearson, and Kozmetsky identify four defining factors:[7]

- It fails to adapt to changing customer needs because it fails to adopt and support the "make-to-order" model for producing customized products and services.
- It attempts to serve the mass market and ends up without a specific value proposition for its customers.
- It fails to get closely involved with its customers because it does not allow them to participate in new product development.
- It implements the traditional strategy of pursuing market share. Today the market is so fragmented that in many sectors every consumer *is* his or her own market segment.

How to Meet Customer Needs: Two Corporate Examples

So how does a company break out of this box and create an offering that completely matches its customers' needs? How does it create a zero value gap?

Two companies have shown how to do so by becoming zero-minded.

Amazon.com

The Amazon.com success story is a textbook example of how zero-minded thinking can result in something unique that truly matches the consumers' requirements. Initially founded as an Internet bookshop, Amazon.com has now expanded to become a site that is dedicated to a total customer experience. Quite simply, it is the place to go for books, CDs, videos, DVDs, and anything else in the world of entertainment. But what is equally important is that Amazon.com makes sure it meets the expectations it creates among its customers. It delivers on time. It gives detailed information about the products offered—even allowing customers to make their own comments—and offers highly competitive discounted prices. For many people, Amazon.com is the first place to go when they need information about books or CDs. There is almost a feeling now that if Amazon.com doesn't have it, then nobody else will either.

FedEx

FedEx has also created its success by looking further than its immediate customer. The question FedEx management asked themselves was what position to take in the total distribution chain. Its customers—the people who called FedEx and asked them to deliver packages—had to operate on the assumption that something sent would actually arrive and arrive on time. Thus, the satisfaction of FedEx's customers depended on the satisfaction of *their* customers. Anybody ordering something wants it quickly. FedEx realized that the satisfaction of the sender—its customer— depended on the satisfaction of the receiver—its customer's customer. By offering an overnight delivery service, it was satisfying the needs of both parties. The ability to deliver this satisfaction—by knowing what the customer's customer wanted—has won FedEx an enormous market share and achieved high customer satisfaction and loyalty.

Strategy has always been preoccupied with finding the right position in a flow of value-creating processes—a position that gives one company rather than a competitor control over its profit-generating capability. But too great a focus on matching and beating the competition leads to reactive, incremental, and often imitative strategic moves—not what is needed in a knowledge-based economy. The irony of competition is this: intense competition makes innovation indispensable, but an obsessive focus on the competition makes innovation difficult to attain.[8]

7

ZERO LEARNING LAG

■ ■ ■ ■ ■ ■ ■ ■ ■ ■ ■ ■ ■ ■ ■ ■ ■ ■ ■ ■

TRAINING PROGRAMS, management courses, seminars: we are inundated with learning opportunities everywhere. This is essential if there is to be a match between the information and knowledge a company has and the work done by its employees. We have long passed the era of the "mushroom management method"—keeping employees in the dark and feeding them mush. But learning is still too often considered an add-on rather than an integral part of the business process.

As we move further into the knowledge-based economy, knowledge and brainpower are given an ever-higher premium. Yet we are also facing a crisis of learning. Rather than producing people well-equipped to enter the new economy, the school systems of both the United States and Western Europe are allowing their standards to drop to worryingly low levels. The new economy is not helped by an old education system!

In an interview in the magazine *Fast Company* John Taylor Gatto said: "Schools . . . are built to supply a mass production economy with a docile workforce; they ask too little of the children, and thereby drain youngsters of curiosity and autonomy."[1]

Today's economy expects exactly that—curiosity and autonomy in employees. Yet the only way many of them know how to learn is based on how they learned in school. And schooling is seldom a model for the sort of ongoing learning that today's knowledge-based economy demands. Formal training can only teach solutions for present training; it cannot induce the zero-mindedness demanded by the new challenges.

Traditional Corporate Training

Training in companies is largely directed at teaching skills that management believes employees should have. It is like dipping a sheep: it immerses the employees in a subject, but most of it is shaken off when they emerge at the other end. Sheep dipping is a very passive activity; it doesn't teach the sheep to take a flea dip as a regular part of its daily life!

But that is exactly what is necessary. Training is often a stop-and-go affair: train today, work tomorrow. This is fine if the need is to improve general performance. But it does little in the way of stopping people from falling behind. It is an incidental action, rather than an integrated part of the business process.

Of course, there is a conviction that employees don't really want to learn; they are perfectly happy to learn just enough to stay up to date. Anything more, it is argued, not only is unwanted but also is wasted energy.

The Internet has turned learning into an adventure. Surfing the Web can be an enriching experience, taking people easily to new knowledge. Why does it seem impossible to mobilize the same interest in learning when we think about business-connected knowledge? Perhaps it is because many believe that training should be done in one's spare time, or should only be considered when there is time to do it.

Yet training and learning are essential. Cisco had fifty people in its training department who were responsible for training about four thousand internal people, plus people in fifteen thousand partner organizations, in not only a rapid stream of new products but also new technologies and Internet-based business practices. This illustrates the challenges that many companies face. "It seemed like an impossible mission: How could this group match the pace of learning at Cisco with the speed of the company's product releases and changes in its markets? And the old approaches—from classroom lectures to multimedia CD-ROMs—seemed hopelessly out of date. Our internal sales force received about 85 percent of its training in the classroom," Tom Kelly, vice president of Cisco worldwide training, marvels. "We are pulling thousands of people out of their jobs, out of contact with their customers, flying them to different locations and shutting them in classrooms for days at a time. It made no sense."[2]

Sound familiar? Of course it does—because it is a problem that every company of any size has to recognize. And most follow the Cisco model of providing immersion training in secluded surroundings.

Ultimately, Keri Pearson distinguishes three types of learning:[3]

- *Rapid learning* occurs in the sort of pressure-cooker courses that are intended to give as much information as possible in as little time as possible. They are usually used to improve general performance.
- In *just-in-time learning* information is provided on a need-to-know-it-now basis. Someone requires a specific skill or piece of information, and he or she is sent away to acquire it.
- *Stealth learning* takes place when learning is built into the work process and is not seen as something isolated from that process. It doesn't require special seminars or long-distance travel; it is fully integrated into the work process, ensuring that people are constantly kept up to speed.

Today, the need for speed must be balanced with the need for zero learning lag. Few companies in this time of rapid change can afford to free their employees for long training sessions. And when they do, they often try to capitalize on the time given by arranging long sessions and a whole mountain of information. In addition, many companies are recognizing the importance of the Net in learning and are investing in e-learning.

AN E-LEARNING JOURNEY AT MERRILL LYNCH

"If a financial consultant is meeting with a client and the topic of discussion is related to material covered in a program that he or she attended several months ago, the key concepts may be remembered, but most likely some of the finer details have been forgotten. We need to provide on-line access to the information in our training program long after the programs are over. Consequently, a lot of what we're dealing with is the structure and classification of information, and we're getting much better at that. It's not just a learning issue; it's a knowledge management issue as well. Financial consultants must have robust remote access training so that they can learn wherever they are, whenever they want."[4]

But even with on-line learning many attempts fail because the design-ers expect people to learn too much at one go. They expect a high atten-tion span when, in fact, we are living in an age of short attention spans. Broadcast news items are carefully edited to last no more than two min-utes. Commercials have to tell their story in just thirty seconds. If we arrive at a site on the Net that doesn't immediately grab our attention, we just click and go.

According to Tom Kelly, "Today people say, 'I'm working,' and what they are doing is quickly answering e-mails and voicemails. They don't say, I've got the next two hours slotted for e-mail. If you do things in small chunks, they become just another part of your job. We want learning to become just another part of your job. E-learning will be successful when it doesn't have its own name."[5]

Learning Innovations

Perhaps one of the greatest obstacles to bridging the learning gap is our desire to compartmentalize work and learning. You are either working or you are out of the process, taking a course. In zero space, that is no longer an option. You cannot divide time up in this way. Instead, if a company is to achieve a zero learning lag, working and learning have to be integrated into one process. People have to move toward what Yeh, Pearson, and Kozmetsky called stealth learning. They have to consider learning and working as two sides of the same coin.

Cisco: Integrating Working and Learning

Cisco's Tom Kelly has been working on this problem since 1997. It is his conviction that "the classroom simply cannot address business issues." The main problem—particularly for a company of Cisco's size—is that a classroom can only hold so many people. How many classes do you have to hold to reach three thousand people every sixty days? "Learning time," says Kelly, "is not a respected part of the work environment. But you can't be so busy that you allow yourself to get stupid. You've got to spend time learning."

Kelly also recognizes that learning cannot be about a set number of hours. These, he believes, are simply arbitrary rules. People learn at different speeds and often not everybody needs to learn the same things. And so, at Cisco, they have introduced assessment tests; this gives an indication of whether and what an employee needs to learn.

Cisco now differentiates between what it calls *structured learning* and *emergency learning*—the stealth learning and just-in-time learning described by Yeh, Pearson, and Kozmetsky. One of the innovations now being introduced is the opportunity for all members of the sales force to create their own Web pages. Each page—with the code name "My Future"—will serve as a learning portal. Employees can chart a long-term structured learning plan, get all relevant short-term updates, and automatically receive the necessary content, based on their job title, area of operation, field of interest, and learning preferences. It will also allow access to time-critical information for emergency learning situations. For example, a salesperson may be required to give a presentation about a new product. That person can download the information and watch it on a laptop or even record it on an MP3 player: instant access to information for instant learning.

Instant Learning: Dell Computer Corporation

So-called instant learning is something that has been developed and implemented very successfully by Dell Computer Corporation. Its 1999 Web site read as follows: "Dell is one of the world's fast-growing computer companies. Our success depends on what we know, what we learn, and how quickly we apply it. And that's where Dell University (Dell U) comes in. Dell U makes learning easier, simpler, faster." Few companies can have placed such a strong emphasis on the need for ongoing learning as a prerequisite for business success!

Yet when Dell University—now Dell Learning—began in 1995, it was not an immediate, unqualified success. It took time for the idea to gain acceptance and support throughout the organization and for the infrastructure needed to be put into place. But the conviction that instant, ongoing learning was an essential strategic tool for Dell made it all happen.

Dell defined four different areas of learning[6]:

- Education required for survival of the company or department
- Education required for the survival of the individual
- Education that would take the company or department to the next level of competence
- Education that would take the individual to the next level of competence

The words used underline the need for ongoing learning. It is a matter of "survival." It must take people "to the next level." It is anything but static; it is continuous.

Dell's instant learning program is based on the Web. People throughout the organization have access to computers that are linked to the Internet. Even employees working in manufacturing can make use of computers located in special kiosks. Programs are developed in direct response to needs from business units—who also foot the bill—and made available on-line. This is a direct extension of Dell's business model—to be "direct"—and encourages employees toward self-direction. Many employees take the initiative to seek out information, expertise, or training as needed. Everybody is made aware of a simple fact: "It's my job to find out."

To ensure that everybody is comfortable with this on-line information access-and-retrieval tool, Dell developed its own program called "Know the Web." Employees may access this program when they desire—it is not mandatory—and people who complete the course receive a poster of Michael Dell, CEO of Dell Computers, with the text: "Michael says I know the Net." It is all part of the instant learning culture, a culture aimed at giving the company a strong strategic advantage: zero learning lag in a zero time environment.

8

ZERO MANAGEMENT
■ ■ ■ ■ ■ ■ ■ ■ ■ ■ ■ ■ ■ ■ ■ ■

ARE MANAGERS IMMUNE to the changes taking place in their markets and their businesses? Obviously not. Yet based on the evidence, it often seems that they are. Training programs are aimed at employees; the higher up in the traditional hierarchy you go, the more you see the urge for empire-building. If the obstacle to a free and ongoing exchange of knowledge is a practical one at the lower levels of an organization, at the management level it is largely intellectual. "Knowing" is seen as a strategic advantage—not necessarily for the company, but for the personal career of the manager concerned.

Managers and a Transient Workforce

As we move into zero space, we must redefine all our existing concepts of organization and management. The old hierarchical mindset has little place in an economy where brainpower is at a premium. Smart professionals know their value and are prepared to make demands that go outside traditional structures in which the lines of responsibility are rigid and working hours and places are regimented.

People today move frequently between companies and industries and inside companies. The workforce is becoming increasingly transient, and consequently organizations lose important elements of permanence. They become more temporary, as reflected in the ad hoc construction of focus groups, project teams, virtual teams, and communities. Such combinations of people will become an increasingly common component of organizational life. As organizations rely on temporary arrangements, management itself will become such an arrangement, and will therefore be limited both in scope and duration: they will become what may be called *disposable leaders*.[1] A person will normally serve as a leader of a group for the duration of a specific assignment or project because he or she has a competence that is important for that particular project.

In such settings, the leadership role can be assumed by another person or the composition of the team can change because of unexpected client demands. People are expected to have many dynamic roles, so a person may simultaneously be the leader of one group and a team member in another. Leaders increasingly become "interchangeable." Bous Shamir introduces the concept of disposable leaders, implying a weakening of the traditional leadership role. He also talks about *teleleadership*, a form of distance leadership that is increasing as corporate locations become more diverse and connected.[2] Certainly this differs from traditional leadership, where making eye contact with followers, inspiring confidence with one's nonverbal behavior, and displaying physical courage or leading through role modeling and personal example are considered essential elements of a proven leader. Now hands-on leaders are becoming on-screen leaders, with all the new problems such virtual leadership implies. Indeed, we might wonder if there is any place for leadership in the emerging organizations. Does zero space mean zero leadership? Are our leaders once again going to move—this time from the shop floor back up to the ivory tower? Do the emerging all-brains, no-body organizations call for a disembodied leadership?[3] Will leaders be required to return to their role of closeted and cosseted managers, issuing directives by e-mail? Or will the diversity and complexity of the knowledge-based economy require a new form of leadership? If so, who will be the brains behind a company that is all brains and no body?

Will leadership really become disposable? Or will the circumstances require leaders to redefine their role and become, in fact, indispensable?

Do "Weakening Situations" Require Strong Leadership?

When organizations become less bounded and more flexible, they become "weak situations." Bureaucratic organizations of the industrial era were "strong situations"—that is, their fixed hierarchies, boundaries, division of labor, rules, regulations, and standard way of operating clearly defined everyone's roles, relationships, and expected behavioral consequences. Thus, they strengthened the situation from the organizational members' point of view. Conversely, weak situations are not uniformly encoded, do not generate uniform expectations about desired behaviors, and do not offer clear incentives contingent upon performance.[4]

Managing Without Managers

As markets, technology, and information move fast, the exchange of knowledge and information must be built into the process. It will be difficult to observe, monitor, capture, exploit, and manage these information and knowledge-exchange processes. As a result, a substantial number of knowledge partners will work without direct supervision. Teams and communities provide a positive way to encourage this exchange—as long as they are not permanent, where each member has his or her own place. Instead, teams must change, with knowledge partners sometimes acting as team leaders and at other times as team members (see Figure 5).

In the figure, the double helix illustrates three important truths about teamwork. First, talent is abundant if we know how to attract, detect, develop, and retain it. Second, people cannot constantly work "in the firing line": even leaders need time to refresh and refocus their efforts. Third, the team has to be responsible for its own performance as best it can inside a larger organizational framework. This new way of working not only allows every part of the company to contain the entire organization's information, knowledge, and capacity for action, but also allows individual professionals to detect and mend gaps in their knowledge, and refresh and refocus their attention, so that they are constantly in learning mode.

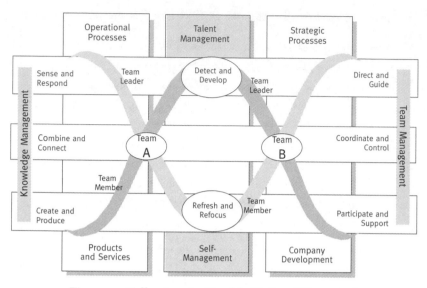

Figure 5. *Following the Double Helix of Teamwork*

Source: R. Tissen, D. Andriessen, and F. Lekanne Deprez, *The Knowledge Dividend: Creating High-Performance Companies Through Value-Based Knowledge Management* (London: Financial Times/Prentice-Hall, 2000), p. 146.

In today's competitive economy, it is no longer sufficient to be competent. Unless one has a desire to learn, competence can easily tip into incompetence—and create a worrisome management gap. It is a constant process of acknowledging that personal improvement, acquisition of personal knowledge, is a key issue for today's professionals. As they thus become knowledge nomads—moving more easily than ever between one company and the next—it is essential that all the explicit knowledge they have and acquire be incorporated into the corporate memory, or corporate IQ.

By now it is obvious that the role of the manager in a process, team, community, and IT-based company is significantly different from the managerial role in a traditional one.

SURVIVAL OF THE SWIFTEST AND THE SMARTEST?

Every existing society, even the most individualistic one, takes two things for granted, if only subconsciously: that organizations outlive workers and that most people stay put. But today the opposite is true. Knowledge workers outlive organizations and they are mobile. The need to manage oneself is creating a revolution in human affairs.[5]

Furthermore (virtual) teams are stimulated to resolve problems and innovate jointly, therefore raising the collective intelligence of organizations. Both corporate memory (knowledge capture) and collective intelligence (knowledge innovation)—and the ease with which both can be constantly updated and accessed—can give the competitive edge.

So What Happens to Managers?

Traditionally, employees became managers only when they had shown that they could operate in a strict, pyramid organization. Once they worked their way up from the base of the pyramid to become manager or director, they had "arrived." Today, once a manager has been appointed, he becomes a sitting duck. Just look at the speed with which management changes. Furthermore, the time that a manager or director serves with a company is becoming ever shorter. A recent report by Drake Beam Morin (DBM), a global human resources firm, reflects the turmoil at the top.[6] The company conducted a global study on executive tenure over the past ten years that specifically targets CEOs. Data on a variety of issues related to CEO tenure were collected from 476 public and private business organizations, including many of the world's largest corporations and representing over fifty different industries in twenty-five countries. The research showed that nearly eight out of ten major companies worldwide had changed their top leader at least once during the 1990s. In just the past five years, close to two-thirds of all major companies had replaced their CEO. Although there is no comparable research from earlier periods, circumstantial evidence and DBM's experience indicate that this is a dramatic increase over earlier decades. DBM found that the CEOs of major corporations today are more likely to lose their jobs as the result of a merger or acquisition than for any other reason. CEO departures caused by such consolidations are, in fact, now nearly ten times more common than departures due to resignation! Another interesting fact is that major companies still tend to look to their own ranks to find replacements for departing CEOs, and in 85 percent of cases select a high-level executive with extensive company experience. Only infrequently—15 percent of the time—do companies recruit a new CEO from outside their organization.

SHAREHOLDERS BEHAVE LIKE SPORTS FANATICS: DITCH THE COACH

Shareholders today are much like football fans. The traditional fan supported his or her club through thick and thin. Nowadays, if their team loses three games in a row, they immediately call for blood: the manager should go! The nightly news offers a familiar picture: the coach, now in a worn raincoat, leaves the stadium for the last time after a "satisfactory and mutually beneficial" discussion with management. The fastest way to satisfy fans is to ditch the coach.

This is also one reason why every self-respecting manager arranges his or her golden parachute in advance, and why managers demand such high salaries. There is little point in planning to stay in a position for a long time because there are always new demands, new competencies required in the person at the top. A new broom is seen as the way to sweep more and better results into the waiting hands of the shareholders. Continuity is no longer provided by people, but by knowledge. So it is essential that this knowledge is shared (in teams, in communities) and stored in the corporate memory.

Changing the Managerial Mindset

There is another problem, however, because top executives are traditionally reluctant to share their knowledge with others. There is still the pervading conviction that knowledge is power and so sharing knowledge reduces that power. There is also the conviction that the knowledge a top executive possesses is his or her most important bargaining chip for future employment. Companies recruit executives simply because they *have* that knowledge. Sharing it would mean their devaluation in the employment market.

This mentality is based on a fundamental misconception: knowledge is something that can be used up. Yet nothing is further from the truth. Sharing knowledge does not mean that one person gets something and the other person loses it. True knowledge sharing is a two-way street; all partners ultimately benefit from it. And the company that employs them benefits as well.

Knowledge sharing must no longer be seen as a kind of giving away of trump cards. Rather, there must be a new determination to create an environment in which such sharing becomes part of the corporate culture. And it can greatly enrich—rather than impoverish—an executive's experience. As a newcomer to a management team, an executive may share his knowledge with four colleagues, but they, in turn, will share four sets of knowledge with him. That's not a bad return on an investment!

When management is constantly changing, there is another advantage: it helps companies break down nonfunctional hierarchies. Traditional old-boy networks and corridors of power are relegated to their proper place in the history books. Status is no longer acquired by position. It is essential that people move effortlessly from one position to another, but doing so requires a new mentality. It is not easy to supervise your colleagues one day and have one of those colleagues become your supervisor the next. People must understand that their competencies, not their personal qualities, place them in a specific position at a specific time. Power—if, indeed, such a term can still be used in organizations that have no hierarchical base—is no longer attached to a person but rather to the knowledge a person may have. And because of the speed with which things change, even that knowledge may provide little basis for continuity. Thus, power structures will need to dissipate as knowledge becomes increasingly the basis for organizations.

9

ZERO RESISTANCE

■ ■ ■ ■ ■ ■ ■ ■ ■ ■ ■ ■ ■ ■ ■ ■

OW OFTEN DO CUSTOMERS want one thing while the corporate process produces another? This mismatch between expectation and performance is one of the main reasons a company loses its competitive edge. Often such mismatches can be traced to bottlenecks and barriers in the corporate process. For example, when a customer requests information from a Web site, that information should be sent out as quickly as possible. A three-week wait for a brochure is unacceptable today, when customers expect instant responses to their demands.

We believe that one of the principal causes for the bottlenecks and barriers is *resistance*.

Dealing with Resistance

People and companies have a built-in resistance to change. Everyone understands the need for change. Everyone knows that it has to happen on an ongoing basis. Yet everyone is also convinced that it's "the other person's" concern. Change, when it happens, always has to begin elsewhere.

This built-in resistance kills change. It is a force that slows or stops movement. It is, once again, like the obstinacy of a mammoth tanker: the pilot turns the wheel to change direction, but it takes a very long time for the tanker to respond. Successful change often is the result of many actions and perspectives at once. Simply continuing on the same course, proceeding "as we have always done," creates an inertia that at times seems almost irresistible.

Yet without change, manufacturers and suppliers are likely to become less and less relevant to customers. Traditionally, manufacturers focused on product deployment and claimed that they listened to "the voice of the customer." Nowadays retailers and other resellers manage the customer interface and the available shelf space. Although manufacturers own the *content* (products, services), the retailer and reseller exert the dominant influence over the *context*.[1] Customers are no longer willing to put up with invisible business processes. They want to judge both the content (the product's life cycle, as with mobile phones) and the context (who provides the best service or return policy). Do manufacturers delight their current and future customers by really delivering their products, services, or processes without any barriers? Instead of focusing on what was achieved this year, a zero resistance approach focuses on what is being done differently this year to delight the customer.

Jeffrey Goldstein, management consultant and professor, believes that resistance simply indicates that the traditional organizational patterns are forcing a system—or way of working—to remain the way it is.[2] In such a context, resistance is expected, accepted, and respected. If we approach change with such a mindset, then we no longer ponder over what causes irresistible resistance but rather on what creates irresistible attraction. If we accept that resistance is inevitable, then rather than flexing our management muscle to force change to happen against the wishes of others, we force ourselves to concentrate on the benefits that will result from change and promote them far more enthusiastically than we normally would think of doing. As the old joke goes: How many psychiatrists are needed to change a lightbulb? Only one—but the lightbulb must be ready to change.

As we said in the last chapter, in the knowledge-based economy successful companies will be those that acknowledge that a sustainable future lies in the ability to share knowledge freely. Such sharing can only occur if there are no bottlenecks, no barriers. Sharing must take place both inside the company and between companies and their partners and stakeholders.

Providing, Organizing, and Directing Knowledge

But knowledge sharing is fundamentally foreign to many companies and employees. Expecting people and companies to share knowledge freely when asked to do so is like expecting an army of frogs to turn into princes on white chargers overnight. Like everything in management and business, some careful thinking and equally careful implementation are needed to get people on the right track.

As shown in Figure 6, the required process includes three fundamental activities: knowledge has to be *provided*, *organized*, and *directed*.

As managing knowledge and focusing efforts to ensure that it adds value increasingly become core tasks of top management—and of all knowledge partners—it will become more important to distinguish between who provides content, who organizes content, and who directs content. It is essential that companies understand the significance of each of these activities and make sure they are carried out by the appropriate

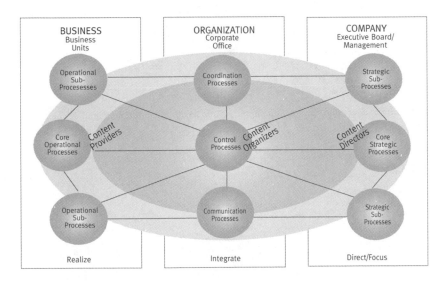

Figure 6. Total Process Organizations

Source: R. Tissen, D. Andriessen, and F. Lekanne Deprez, *The Knowledge Dividend: Creating High-Performance Companies Through Value-Based Knowledge* Management (London: Financial Times/Prentice Hall, 2000), p. 140.

business units. The business units that are nearest the market and responsible for operational matters are the primary *content providers*. They are also responsible for operational knowledge management, connecting systems to people and vice versa. The corporate center acts as the *content organizer*, often using IT to carry out this task. Its importance lies in its "return on interaction" and decision support. In other words, corporate center staff positions—such as marketing and business development—support the units rather than have assigned responsibilities. Top management is the *content director* and strategically focuses on the value it needs to add to the company. With the expansion of IT as enabler—or even driver—throughout the organization, the corporate center's role will probably diminish in the future. Already, many IT networks are directly connecting operational and strategic processes (both internal and external). Employees in such organizations become co-creators of value. Even customers have a hand in the creation of services, products, and processes. All this implies that intelligence (valuable content) flourishes in a networked world.

CORPORATE OFFICES: CO-CREATORS OF VALUE?

The traditional thinking is that only business units—not the corporate office—create value for a company. In their examination of four corporations—Sprint, WPP, Teradyne, and Viacom—Michael Raynor and Joseph Bower found that the corporate office can create value by assembling a portfolio of assets and capabilities that will drive competition in the future and managing those assets in a flexible way so as not to hinder the ability of the divisions to compete now.[3]

KEY QUESTIONS FOR MANAGERS IN A NETWORKED WORLD

"Conceptualize your organization as a network with a core (back end) and a periphery (front end). At the back end, can you centralize processes that are shared across different business units to create an internal 'utility company?' Can you convert dedicated infrastructure by pushing some business processes beyond the walls of the organization to external utility companies? At the front end, can you get closer to your customers and partners by pushing intelligence nearer to them?"[4]

The whole flow-through process must be continuous: customer satisfaction leads to feedback, which in turn is used as input for strategic management processes, core business processes, and resource management processes. This input from the market acts like a litmus test when companies decide on the strategic necessity or advantage offered by alliances or other relationships.

Furthermore, these alliances and relationships must be constantly reassessed for their contribution to the core products and services that the customer demands. Only when the process is continuous, with input from the customer determining everything that a company does, can barriers be eliminated and the zero space organization achieved.

10

ZERO EXCLUSION

■ ■ ■ ■ ■ ■ ■ ■ ■ ■ ■ ■ ■ ■ ■ ■

I N TODAY'S WORLD companies are competitors in the morning, partners in the afternoon, and friends at night. Peter Senge and Goran
Carstedt believe that "our real future lies in building sustainable enterprises and an economic reality that connects industry, society, and the environment."[1] Leadership in the twenty-first century is a matter of inspiring,
motivating, and challenging people, many of whom are *not* employed by
the leading enterprise and not under the influence of formal leadership.
Leaders must be able to trust and "let loose" the operations of partners and
employees, without having full control over them. What worked well when
those companies were going it alone may not work in a collaborative environment. The competencies needed for leaders to make progress are co-
sensing (jointly "tuning into" emerging patterns) and co-creating the new.[2]
Often there is not a lot of time to comanufacture or coevolve. In high-
velocity markets, leaders neglect to update their collaborative links as businesses and markets emerge, grow, split, and combine.[3] They become
OECs—*O*perating on the *E*dge of *C*haos—instead of CEOs.[4]

To succeed in the knowledge-based economy, companies know they
must gather around them a group of complementary and supporting
forces. In today's process- and pace-driven companies—in which bottlenecks have been eliminated to ensure greater customer satisfaction and
retention—any weak link in the process chain can prove disastrous. The
failure of a supplier to produce parts on time or the failure of the distribution network to act promptly and accurately can create dissatisfaction.
As CEO Michael Dell explains: "If you don't create an integrated value
chain, don't expect to survive."[5]

A LITTLE KNOWLEDGE OF THE WRONG KIND IS A DANGEROUS THING

The pitfalls of a traditional value chain were further highlighted by Michael Dell when he noted that the feedback system in the "old" automobile distribution value chain could actually lead to misinformation. "If you have three yellow Mustangs sitting on a dealer's lot and a customer wants a red one, the salesman is really good at figuring out how to sell a yellow Mustang. So the yellow Mustang gets sold, and a signal gets sent back to the factory that, hey, people want yellow Mustangs," Dell explained.[6]

Often such problems arise because process participants are excluded from the process.

It is obvious that any rigid organization will not attain the flexibility, adaptability, and agility required to meet the changing conditions companies are facing on the outside. We are reminded of the old fable of the oak and the reed: the rigid strength of the oak proved its ultimate downfall. A dogged adherence to old organizational forms and theories will ultimately have a similar effect.

LIVING IN ECO-SPACE

Eco-space—that is, the environment—is made up of *stocks* of resources and *sinks* for wastes. In other words, it contains a stock of resources for us to exploit as well as sinks to absorb our wastes. Eco-space measures the sustainable carrying capacity of these stocks and sinks.[7]

The Integrated Process Chain

Exclusion is often a leftover from the industrial economy. Purchasing departments that simply request quotations from suppliers, beat down costs, impose supply conditions, and ignore agreed payment terms do little to encourage suppliers to think and act like partners. Although most managers understand that including suppliers in the "inner circle" can be for the good of all concerned, they also acknowledge the established power and autonomy of such departments. Yet it is important—indeed vital— for them to understand that they are no longer *in* logistics—or marketing, purchasing, IT, or consulting—but *between* them.

Suppliers

Suppliers today are a vital link in the process chain. It is simply impossible, with the speed of change and the need for fluidity and flexibility, to do everything without their willing and dedicated participation. Partnerships—a word that has been bandied about for years, but whose implications seem lost on many companies stubbornly remaining in the industrial economy—are the lifeblood of any enterprise. Comakership is not an aim but rather a necessity. Including everybody in the process—creating zero exclusion—is simple common sense; exclusion is simple suicide.

Customers

Nor must this concept apply only to suppliers; customers too must be included. Some thirty years have passed since futurist Alvin Toffler coined the term *prosumer*: customers who actively participate in generating the value they derive from any product, service, or process. In the future, producers will own forever what they produce and therefore will have strong incentives to design products to be disassembled and remanufactured or recycled, whichever is more economical. But how will a company think of itself in relation to its customers? As a producer of things that people buy or a provider of services through products that are made and remade? When a company (Volvo, for example) only sells cars, its relationship with the customer ends with the purchase. But when it provides customer satisfaction, its relationship just begins with that purchase![8]

Customers' Customers

We have already seen that it is essential to create a continuous process in which customer input is used to develop new products and services and determine strategic alliances and relationships. Indeed, it is also essential for a company to know its customer's customers. Only then can it create a zero value gap in which expectations are met.

When Cisco announced a $2.2 billion inventory write-down in the second quarter of 2001, skeptics immediately heralded the fall of the "inclusive" network business model that Cisco exemplifies. Cisco was just as vulnerable as any other company to an economic slowdown. Once upon a time, the massless high-techs Cisco and Nortel Networks were taking over the world. Now the network orchestrators are experiencing their first real taste of adversity, but—according to Remo Häcki and Julian Lighton—the network strategies they deploy look stronger than ever.[9] But perhaps the most important lesson comes from looking behind the numbers. These high-tech companies, which sell telecom equipment, clearly misread the market, in part because they weren't analyzing their *customers' business*. Most of their sales came from alternative phone companies that had relied on venture capitalists and Wall Street for funding equipment purchases rather than using cash flow from their operations. When that money abruptly dried up, the shortfall drove many of the new phone companies out of business.[10]

Recognizing the Business Ecosystem

As we have seen, Intel is intensely concerned with all aspects of its process. Intel considers its entire market as an ecosystem. It shares information with its distributors and with the chief information officers of large companies—in other words, with its customers' customer.

The concept of the business ecosystem has also been discussed by Roger Lewin and Birute Regine and by James F. Moore.[11,12]

According to Lewin and BRegine, "It is possible to think of any business ecosystem in terms of a network of companies, each occupying a place in its own landscape of possibilities, and each landscape being coupled to many others: those of competitors, collaborators, and complementers. As the landscape of one of the companies changes—perhaps through a leapfrogging innovation—the landscapes of those connected to it will also change: some will increase in size, while others get smaller, or even disappear."[13]

The objective of the traditional corporation is to manage one or more operating business units so that they grow revenues and profits, and so that they live long. This form of organization focuses managers' attention on two things: their core markets and their core operations. According to Moore, the problem with this model is that it creates in managers a corresponding blindness to developments occurring outside their core. That is, the "white space" between existing markets and operations is left, to a large extent, unattended. Yet in a global economy with ample free capital, talented knowledge partners, and technological inventiveness, much of the opportunity facing businesses originates in the white space. This is true whether one is seeking to extend one's existing business or develop new ones.

Lewin and Regine continue: "The benefits include the opportunity to reap great rewards through the economics of increasing returns and through forming alliances or other forms of partnerships. But when everything is connected directly or indirectly to everything else, changes in one part of the system may be propagated throughout the web of connections, and sometimes organizations become extinct through no fault of their own."[14]

Today, organizations must become disorganized. They cannot continue creating rigid structures to serve a very flexible market. Thinking functionally and carefully drawing boundaries around each individual area of business activity can only create exclusion. And exclusion will ultimately lead to extinction.

We believe that nonexclusion is the ultimate aim. Unless managers take radical steps to exclude exclusion from their business thinking, they will become business dinosaurs: all body and very little brain. And we all know the fate suffered by those prehistoric reptiles.

11

ZERO TECH

Z ERO TECH? You are surely saying that technology is everywhere, so how can we talk about zero tech? And of course, you are right. Technology is everywhere. But we are convinced that zero tech will happen when computing and technology become so ubiquitous that they are simply taken for granted. Indeed, we are gradually approaching that phase today.

Ubiquitous Computing

The term *ubiquitous computing* was first coined by Mark Weiser in 1988.[1] The concept places technology on the periphery of our lives, rather than at the center. It becomes a tool, something we use. It does not require our attention, it is just there. Like the information system in a modern airport, it is where we want it when we want it. Airport information relies on a sophisticated IT network, in which enormous amounts of data are processed and exchanged with only one aim in mind: to give passengers the information they need. It is ubiquitous, not an end in itself but a means to an end.

When businesses become zero-minded about technology they can concentrate on what they should be doing: finding ways to add value to their operations and to the lives and work of their customers. But how tempting it is to concentrate on other things! Do we need the Internet? Do we need a LAN? Do we need . . . ? Of course, in the knowledge-based economy, the answer is always yes. But we have to get beyond such technology-based issues and put technology in its proper place. When we put the ignition key into our car and turn it, we don't expect to have seventeen committee meetings to decide if the car should start!

Today, technology is invading every area of our lives. The digital revolution has been fought and won. There are chips in everything—from computers to televisions, telephones, vacuum cleaners, and cameras. New products for connecting us to information are springing up like daffodils in spring. And many of these will become embedded in the fabric of our lives—contributing to them, but working, almost, in the background.

Obviously there is a flipside to all this. Thoughts of Big Brother almost automatically arise. The ubiquitous computer can track our every move—or almost. We are placed in restaurants, because we used our credit card there. Or on a plane. Or in a hotel. Technology can also monitor our computer usage, our e-mails.

Indeed, these are the dangers when ubiquitous computing is part of our environment. The computer provides the frame in which we live. Privacy issues come to the fore: a computer that registers one's every movement, preferences, decisions, and actions, and makes this information available to anybody else, is certainly a frightening prospect. Linking existing, separate databases poses similar problems. And there is the difficulty of creating personalized information in such a ubiquitous computing environment. The worst scenario would mean inputting personal data into every new device every time one changes jobs.

An alternative concept—and one that is gaining momentum—is the wearable computing system. Why place cameras and detectors in a room when the person entering that room could be wearing these devices instead? Wearable computing facilitates a new form of human-computer interaction based on a small computer system worn on the body that is always on, always ready, always accessible. This new computational framework differs from handheld devices, laptops, or personal digital assistants (PDAs). The always-ready capability leads to a new synergy between human and computer based on long-term adaptation because of constant interface.[2] The MIThril project vision, at the MIT Media Lab in Massachusetts, is that wearable computing is technology people live with. It is synergistic, flexible, and adaptable to a wide range of circumstances.[3] The vision behind such a system is that a mobile computer should not just be a machine that we take with us when we plan to do some work on the road. Instead, it becomes an integral part of our everyday clothing. Imagine a tourist arriving in a foreign city. As soon as she leaves the train, her wearable computer contacts the local tourist office and compiles a list of suitable hotels nearby. It then guides her to the chosen hotel. The directions are integrated in her view of the real world via a computer display in her sunglasses. The display also shows information on landmarks and restaurants she passes on her way to the hotel. At the same time, the computer informs her about local customs or hazards that she should be aware of (such as to be careful in this area after dark).[4]

How far away are such wearable systems? Perhaps nearer than we think. Already there are mobile phones that pack a hefty computing punch. Some offer download facilities for MP3 files, allowing users to listen to music over their mobile phone. If a phone call comes in, it immediately takes priority. Palmtop organizers are almost as powerful as laptops. And laptops are certainly a match for desktops.

Ubiquitous Systems and Too Much Control

A very real and present danger is that, as computing systems become ubiquitous, they may be used to monitor the activities of knowledge workers. When did they log on? When did they log off? What was their output? For how long did they meet with a certain client? How long were they stuck in a traffic jam? The specter, already featured in Hollywood movies, of a supervisor constantly checking the length of a salesman's phone pitch has become a reality and a very real problem. The greater the control, the less the freedom, and therefore the less the job satisfaction. Piecework was common in the industrial economy. Will it soon make an entrance into the knowledge-based economy?

We can already stay in contact with everybody all the time. The ringing of mobile telephones on ski slopes is a more joyous sound for many of today's executives than a trumpet fanfare. ("They simply can't get along without me.") Keep in touch? We are gradually entering a time when the ultimate power will be to decide to be *out* of touch.

The introduction of the electronic highway, laptops, palmtops, wireless modems—you name it—has given people a greater freedom to work whenever and wherever they want to. But it has also extended the workday. Leaving the office no longer means leaving work. People take their work with them, wherever they go. On boats and planes and trains, in cars and subways, in restaurants and even bathrooms. "Smile, you're *on-line!*" In effect, these devices can create a kind of portable assembly line that allows "wired-collar workers" to remain on-line and accessible anytime, anywhere, at any place.

Today, there is much discussion about the corporation's growing responsibility—toward ethics in business, toward the environment, toward developing countries. The exploitation of cheap sweatshop labor is condemned, even if it is kept alive by companies seeking the very lowest production costs. *Responsibility* and *accountability* are words heard frequently in discussions about corporate government.

Does zero tech imply that we are moving into a "sweatshop" knowledge environment? We hope not. In fact, we believe that when technology no longer has our undivided attention, we will be freed to exploit brainpower in a responsible and accountable way.

In a speech, Shimon Peres, Israel's Minister of Regional Cooperation, said: "The moment you go from an economy of land to an economy of brains, you don't have real borders. You have, instead, horizons that you can never reach. Every time you try to reach them, you discover another horizon—higher, more promising, farther away, unsolved, always inviting. This is not just the globalization of the economy but rather the globalization of the young generation. I believe today the division is not as much between left and right as between an outgoing generation and an incoming generation."[5]

Shifting the Focus from Technology to People

As we move toward zero tech, we can allow our focus to shift from technology to people. Indeed, people remain the heart of organizations. But with the advent of new technologies, it seems that they are being lost in the background. The two figures shown here contrast what happens when technology rules and when people retain control.

When technology is allowed to rule (see Figure 7), business processes become standardized. In consequence, more protocols and procedures are introduced. This means that people have to work in a fixed framework.

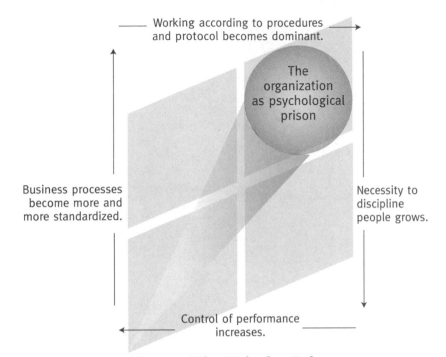

Working according to procedures
and protocol becomes dominant.

The
organization
as psychological
prison

Business processes
become more and
more standardized.

Necessity to
discipline
people grows.

Control of performance
increases.

Figure 7. *When Technology Rules*

Source: M. Proos and O. Wiegel, *The Digital Avenue* (master's thesis) (Breukelen, The Netherlands: Nyenrode University), p. 59.

Control over performance increases because output is standardized and easy to measure. In addition, a stricter disciplinary regime is required because standardization demands uniformity.

In contrast, when people retain control (see Figure 8), the effectiveness of the company increases. People are empowered and learn the joy and benefits of being involved and committed. There's an increasing feeling of togetherness in the way work gets done. People do not consider themselves prisoners chained into organizational structures and systems. The organization becomes a platform for innovation.

Although computers can already perform some types of human brainwork—and will be able to do more of it in the future—organizations must focus on human intelligence and competencies. Innovation and creativity come from extraordinary people, not from computers. Organizations are cracking the code of change. Taking standardization one step too far brings back the old way of doing things: bureaucratically.

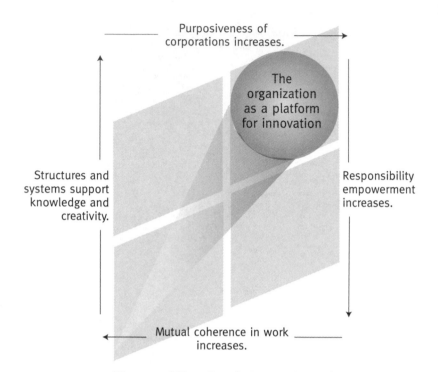

Figure 8. *When People Retain Control*

Source: M. Proos and O. Wiegel, *The Digital Avenue* (master's thesis) (Breukelen, The Netherlands: Nyenrode University), p. 59.

Employees must not be put into the straitjacket of standardization. Otherwise, as process failures emerge, they will not be able to, or not be allowed to, release the power within them to overcome these failures, or even better, to anticipate failures and prevent them from happening.

So organizations must empower people. To create an innovative environment, systems and structures must support knowledge sharing and stimulate creativity. Project teams, which are common in virtual organizations, will lead to more mutual coherence and a greater focus on goals. This is what today's fast-changing markets demand.

In the future, IT systems will be more flexible and better at anticipating new developments. Integration with different sources and systems will become easier. The demand for standardization will disappear.

If technology is allowed to rule, it could end up creating a knowledge prison, which would eventually lead to a lack of initiative, decreased speed and flexibility, and a lethargy that has no place in zero space. When people are allowed to rule, then what could have been a prison suddenly becomes a springboard for new thoughts, new ideas, new horizons, and new successes.

Become zero-minded about technology. Allow people to occupy their minds once again. For they possess the brainpower that can lead to the great ideas that will make your company successful.

PART III

Launching into Zero Space

12

ZEROING IN ON
REALITY

■ ■ ■ ■ ■ ■ ■ ■

I**N THE CHAPTERS IN PART II** we examined the building blocks of the zero space organization and the obstacles to achieving the sort of flexibility and customer service that spells success in the knowledge-based economy. In this chapter we look at the changes that a company must consider in order to launch itself into zero space.

Changing the Managerial Mindset

One of the greatest obstacles to the organizational changes that must happen is in the managerial mindset. As we discussed in earlier chapters, managers who build their careers and achieve success, power, authority, and respect become convinced that "the more you know, the higher you rise." Sharing knowledge is not a sign of strength, but of weakness.

But this, of course, is in sharp contrast to the zero-mindedness required for success in zero space. It will continue to be a stumbling block unless managers realize that they must not only initiate change but also participate in it. At the same time, employees must realize that change is essential if they are to gain ongoing satisfaction and fulfillment from their work and they must also try to remain flexible and adaptable to emerging needs.

To realize zero-mindedness throughout the organization, it is not enough to tinker with the structure, removing layers here, improving consultation there, or encouraging knowledge exchange between managers. Such minor adaptations to a faulty structure will not improve it at all; they will be little more than cosmetic improvements.

As we pointed out throughout the first parts of this book, the old hierarchical management structure of the industrial economy has no place in the knowledge-based economy.

IN PRAISE OF HIERARCHY?

"Hierarchy is not to blame for our problems. What we need is not simply a new, flatter organization but an understanding of how managerial hierarchy functions: how it relates to the complexity of work and how we can use it to achieve a more effective deployment of talent and energy. . . . If we are to make our hierarchies function properly, it is essential to place the emphasis on *accountability for getting work done*. This is what hierarchical systems ought to be about. Authority is a secondary issue and flows from accountability in the sense that there should be just that amount of authority needed to discharge the accountability. So if a group is to be given authority, its members must be held accountable as a group, and unless this is done, it is very hard to take so-called group decisions seriously."[1]

Lines of authority and complicated consultation processes make no contribution whatsoever to zero speed. In today's rapidly changing marketplace, the competition will already have gotten up and gone before the date of the second meeting has even been agreed on. Indeed, in the industrial economy, when all is said and done, more is said than done. We must change from being meeting managers to action managers: managers who do not have to organize a series of meetings "to bring everybody up to speed" but rather incorporate an ongoing, instant, and reliable exchange of ideas and information into the working process.

In chapter 4, on zero matter, we saw that success does not depend on owning knowledge but on benefiting from it. This implies a flexibility, a fluidity, a readiness to adapt instantly so that the knowledge that is required now can be accessed now.

Employing Teams

Many companies that are already inspired by process thinking, described in chapter 9, have turned to teams to create small flexible units that can act as microcosms of the company. Teams provide a way of working together across functional barriers and concentrating with greater focus on customer satisfaction and leveraging the knowledge of the team. *Teamwork* is the watchword.

Yet often—almost inevitably, it seems—teams lose their flexibility almost as soon as they are created. Team members find their own place on the team, leaders emerge, and soon the existing hierarchical structure reimposes itself.

We believe that many teams are created without a clearly defined task. Often we read about a "quality team," an "organization team," a "you-think-of-a-title" team. "Let's create a team," is the feeling, "and then everything will turn out fine."

But teams need to focus on a single task. They should be created when needed and then disbanded when that task is accomplished. A team must be created to achieve a specific task; tasks should not be developed to keep a team busy.

Still, the more important question to ask is this: Do teams really provide a basis for a true zero space organization? We do not think they do—at least, not if they are the destination rather than the point of departure. Yet it is obvious that teams drawn from different functional areas are crucial stepping-stones to the drastic process of change that is required in both organizations and mindsets.

Dealing with Instability in a Virtual World

The rapid advances in IT have changed the geography of the business environment. Companies are becoming less confined in their operations. It is now possible—and quite common—to have R&D facilities in various centers throughout the world, production centers on other continents, and a virtual shop that can be accessed by anyone with a computer and an Internet connection. Knowledge partners work wherever they happen to be. E-mail addresses take the place of physical addresses. Teams are no longer made up of people you see face to face, people no longer attend meetings in one place—they attend meetings wherever they happen to be, regardless of where the other participants are located. "The right place at the right time" is now simply "the right time."

In the virtual world we are moving toward there is no tangible home base. Is it surprising, then, that people are becoming disoriented? It is always a comfortable feeling to know where you fit in. In many companies, promotion meant moving one's office to a higher floor. How can people enjoy the trappings of success if they have nothing to show for it? *It simply doesn't make sense.*

This feeling of instability is only strengthened in a world in which speed and agility rule. And it was aggravated further when companies that once seemed to offer the most promise for the future suddenly faced oblivion. The collapse of NASDAQ companies proved just how ephemeral success is. Suddenly the golden boys of the knowledge-based economy—the dot-coms—were revealed as naked emperors. They were forced to acknowledge that they no longer had the power to print money. They had to work for it like any other company.

THE WAR FOR TALENT IS ENTERING THE COMBAT ZONE

Hostility greets most of the Dutch former partners of McKinsey & Company who want to return to the fold after a failed adventure into Internet territory—not the sort of reception they were expecting. But McKinsey publicly expresses its indifference to the wanderers by rejecting nine out of ten who reapply for their old jobs. "We are not a safety net for failed entrepreneurs," says Robert Reibestein, director of McKinsey Netherlands, as he sentences them to lifelong banishment. Why amid this amazing display of loyalty one consultant out of every ten is allowed readmittance is a mystery. And have all the rejects failed to learn from their adventure, which should make them all the more valuable than before? After all, experience is the name everyone gives to their mistakes.[2]

Many executives who had been promised the golden egg found that they had been goosed instead. The market value of dot-coms was based on future returns. They promised enormous riches, pointing to the success of the likes of Amazon.com and shouting that "anything they can do, we can do better."

FOREVER MANAGING AFTERMATH: DO WE EVER LEARN?

"The history of the industrial economy is strewn with companies that, once bright new lights, have since faded into obscurity, senescence, or death because their leaders managed in the past imperfect tense—that is, forever managing aftermath. They became bureaucracies: businesses that existed to run organizations. The way out of this dead end is in finding new models of managing in the new economy."[3]

The sudden demise of companies that spent $3 in promotion for every $1 of sales was a red light for the corporate world. Was the Internet really the promised land? Was virtual reality any reality at all?

It is not surprising that this vast miscalculation—a miscalculation that had tempted some of the most promising talent in business to risk all—should have sown the seeds of discontent and disbelief. Why did it happen?

Of course there is no single explanation. Some people believe that investors got tired of being paid in promises rather than hard cash. Others believe that although the dot-com pioneers did the scouting, the large corporations stepped in and started playing the game by their rules. And they were better at it.

In corporate life today many of the dot-com wonder boys are returning to the fold of old economy companies. But they have seen the promised land and few are willing to give up the vision entirely. They may, like Moses, not be allowed to enter but they know what it looks like. And it *doesn't* look like a nine-to-five job behind the same old desk. It *doesn't* look like the same old hierarchical structure.

The biggest task for companies today is to find a way to balance ambiguity and clarity, to create flexibility and stability, and to enter zero space.

Where Are We Now?

It's all very well to speak of the old and new economies, of the industrial economy and the knowledge-based economy; indeed, in a book of this nature doing so is unavoidable. But it creates the impression that there is some clearly visible demarcation between them, where the one stops and the other begins. But the truth is different. It is more like driving from Los Angeles to Las Vegas: at one point you cross the border between California and Nevada, but you're still in the desert. There is, it would seem, a no-man's land in which you are in neither one nor the other, or rather in both.

Many business analysts have commented on this phenomenon. We are all desperate to "get into" the knowledge-based economy but we want to take a lot of the old economy baggage with us. We want to have the best of both worlds. We prepare to move into the knowledge-based economy but continue running our business in old economy mode—just in case! And the situation is made even more complex by the fact that many of the clients of new economy companies are themselves still more comfortable in the tried-and-tested surroundings of the old economy.

For example, companies—and their employees and shareholders—are often suspicious of outsiders. Secret agreements, entrance controls, espionage alerts, patents, and "we've got something you haven't got" are part of an atmosphere that hardly sets the scene for the knowledge-based economy, in which sharing, alliances, partnerships, joint ventures, and networks are the order of the day. How can people who have looked at the competition as "the enemy" be expected to embrace them as friends and allies? To make things even more complex, how can they be expected to treat them as allies at one moment, competitors the next, and partners the next? Indeed, on some occasions, they may be all of these at the same time!

Dealing with the Virtual Corporation

The term *virtual corporation* was first coined by *Business Week* in 1993: "The virtual corporation will seem to be a single entity with vast capabilities but will really be the result of numerous collaborations assembled only when they're needed."[4]

This phrase had its origins in the world of computers where the term *virtual memory* was used to imply that the computer had more storage capacity than it really possessed—an electronic sleight-of-hand. Today, *virtual* has achieved a meaning all its own. We have virtual reality and virtual shopping, and virtually anything else can be virtual.

It was A. Mowshowitz who first used the term *virtual organization*.[5] Recently, he updated his definition:

> *In virtual memory a distinction is made between physical and logical storage space. . . . Programmers using such a system need not concern themselves with the actual physical space assigned to their programs. Indeed, virtual memory was developed in connection with time-sharing so that the physical location of a program—instructions, data, intermediate results— may be* switched *from moment to moment under control of the operating system. The table of correspondences between physical and logical space keeps track of the changes.*[6]

This *switching principle* is certainly very much applicable to zero space organizations. Companies are expected to react to new situations in zero time, switching their attention from one business area to another, from one market to another, from one challenge to another, from one opportunity to another. What's more, this switching principle is also applicable to alliances and partnerships—here this morning, gone this afternoon. It implies a fluidity of action, a flexibility in mindset, and a total lack of rigidity in the organization.

But Mowshowitz's definition also includes another vital element for today's organizations: connection. Indeed, connectivity may be at the very heart of companies operating in the knowledge-based economy. Certainly the pervasive use of IT has radically altered the business landscape. It has allowed people greater freedom to work when and where they want to. It has helped companies extend their boundaries into areas—both business and geographic—that may otherwise have remained closed to them. But there is also a hidden danger: many companies embark on ambitious IT programs without first fully understanding their present physical organization. Thus IT becomes nothing more than a fix—it is doubtful that it will have any lasting benefits.

All companies revolve around three principles: *ownership*, *power*, and *loyalty*.[7] In traditional industrial and service companies, there is unity among all three areas. Unity of ownership implies that there are no internal divisions, no conflicts of interest. Unity of power ensures a direction for the company and a way to resolve conflicts. And unity of loyalty is often seen as a fundamental asset for many industrial companies.

In a zero space organization, there is no longer any unity in these principles. Ownership is anything but clear-cut; it is distributed between a constantly changing number of stakeholders and can thus become a source of conflict of interest between the various owners. It also has an immediate influence on power: this, too, is distributed, and can once again become a source of conflict. If these conflicts are not solved immediately, they can result in a connection paralysis and even the withdrawal of key participants. Loyalty is distributed too: employees are expected to show loyalty not only to their "own" company but also to partner companies. But it is a short-lived loyalty, unlike the ongoing loyalty that is a characteristic of traditional companies. The challenge that management faces—and, indeed, that employees face too—is how to engender internal and external loyalty—that is, from customers—in a fragmented business environment.

Is Your Company Physical or Virtual?

It is always tempting to think in an "either/or" way. An organization is either physical or virtual. But the truth, as always, lies somewhere in between. No company can exist totally in a virtual world—and those that have tried (including some of the more famous dot-com ventures) have learned the contrary to their regret. Ultimately products need to be made, distributed, and used. The question is not whether a company is virtual or physical but rather whether the operations lend themselves in a greater or lesser degree to "virtualization."

A zero space organization must be flexible, agile, and adaptable. Tomorrow's circumstances may require a greater or lesser degree of virtualization. This is why we see everything as a continuum, for a continuum implies the ability to change and adapt.

This should not imply that zero space is less applicable to one end of the scale than the other. We do not believe that zero-mindedness is an option; it is a necessity. However, although the principles are valid across the board, they will never result in any one, single, ideal organization. Organizations are highly personal things, almost as personal as fingerprints. It is vital that managers understand the true nature of their business and allow their organization to develop as a unique reflection of the company itself.

A virtual organization focuses on delivering customized information, knowledge, goods, and services when and where they are needed. Yet there is a continuous blurring of boundaries. Where does one company end and another begin? As suppliers and distributors become partners rather than simple members of the supply chain, the identities of companies are in danger of becoming equally blurred. And there is the ever-present danger of a loss of proprietary knowledge. Certainly as more—and changing—partners have access to essential knowledge, the possibility of its loss increases. Thus, in zero space successful companies will not necessarily own knowledge but will understand how to benefit from it.

The Four Aspects of Zero Space Organizations

To enter zero space—and operate successfully in zero time, with zero matter, zero value gap, zero learning lag, zero management, zero resistance, zero exclusion, and zero tech—organizations will have four features. They will be network-based, partnership-based, community-based, and IT-centric. In the next four chapters we look at each of these features in detail.

CREATING ZERO SPACE AREAS IN ORGANIZATIONS

"By retaining a certain level of ambiguity, the organization provides the white space within which members can play, experiment, and improvise. When ambiguity is excessively high, people are confused and anxious, because they lack a frame of reference to interpret their work and actions for the organization. On the other hand, when ambiguity is unduly suppressed, people become complacent and unwilling to experiment or change, shielded as they are from the need to adapt. Each organization finds its own balance between ambiguity and certainty, the particular locus depending on the business of the organization, its relationships with other institutions and stakeholders, its external environment, and its cultural ethos."[8]

13

NETWORKING WITH
NETWORKS

■ ■ ■ ■ ■ ■ ■ ■ ■ ■

THERE HAS ALWAYS BEEN something suspect about networks. The word suggests exclusive clubs, sects almost, to which entrance is not by ability but by circumstance: the old boys' network, the golf club network. Membership is taken for granted by those who "belong" and looked upon with envy by those who are excluded. There are even networks of directors, without whose help things rarely used to get done in business.

Today, that negative association is receding. Managers understand that all organizations are part of a greater whole. They exist thanks to relationships, associations, and connections. There are relationships with stakeholders—whether they are employees, suppliers, customers, or shareholders. Indeed, any company that cannot boast a recurring network of associations is unlikely to exist very long.

Types of Networks

According to James R. Lincoln, professor at the University of California, "To assert that an organization is not a network is to strip it of that quality in terms of which it is best defined: the pattern of recurring linkages."[1] This definition—a pattern of recurring linkages—applies at all organizational levels. There are links within teams or departments or business units, links between suppliers and customers, links between disciplines, links between customers and markets and between innovation and R&D. Many of these links—these networks—are formal. There are contracts with suppliers, for example. There are (one hopes) long-term, ongoing relationships with customers. Other links are more ad hoc, such as teams, for, as we discussed in the previous chapter, teams should change with changing circumstances.

Often forgotten, however, are informal networks. These hidden networks can be of incalculable value. The value of an employee's contacts is often underestimated, and it is not knowing the "right" people that counts. Rather, it is knowing the right person to provide the appropriate complementary knowledge at any given moment. It is not a network of "like minds" but rather a network of "unlike minds." A network of people with dissimilar knowledge is of far greater value than a network of people with the same ideas. It's not a question of whom you know but rather a question of what is known by the people you know!

Any organization is not just a network in itself. In fact, it can be seen as a network of other organizations. The person who coined the phrase *World Wide Web* showed remarkable insight into the interlinking that is happening in the world today. As author Stephen R. Barley so graphically put it, "Not only are organizations suspended in multiple, complex, and overlapping webs of relationships, but the webs are likely to exhibit structural patterns that are invisible from the standpoint of a single organization caught in the tangle. To detect overarching structures, one has to rise above the individual firm and analyze the system as a whole."[2]

The first aspect of zero space organizations is that they are network-based. They must understand the intrinsic value of networks. But they must also realize that networks are as subject to change as anything else in business. Networks that work today may no longer work tomorrow. Newly emerging networks may radically change existing ones. This must be accepted as a normal part of business life. Attempting to retain networks because "they have always been like that" is a recipe for disaster.

Characteristics of Networked Organizations

Despite the diversity of today's networked organizations, several characteristics seem common to them all.[3]

Common Objectives

First, networked organizations have common objectives. They are all mov-ing toward the same goal—a goal that needs to be understood and accepted by everybody. This is not to say there is uniformity or even con-sensus about how these goals should be achieved or the best route to take to reach them. Rather, the objectives are shared; each part of the network must then devise its own strategy and direction.

Shared Knowledge

Second, a networked organization shares knowledge and expertise. It must be prepared to share or it will simply not be able to exist. As we have already said, it is essential in this sharing to create a synergy in which knowledge and ideas are seen as complementary and challenging. Tradi-tionally, many companies grew by doing everything themselves—acquir-ing knowledge and expertise for their exclusive use. In zero space, such thinking must be a thing of the past. It is no longer a question of owning knowledge or trying to acquire knowledge for personal and exclusive use; rather it is necessary to develop ways in which the benefits of knowledge can be enjoyed. Ideally, any network should provide access to the knowl-edge and expertise needed *now*. This implies a constant rejuvenation of the network as one area of expertise is acquired and another discarded.

But in zero space there is yet another dimension: networks allow con-nections between geographic locations often on different continents. The time has passed when expertise needs to be brought to a central location; instead, we are witnessing the use of expertise wherever it happens to be. Gone are the days when the CEO ordered: "If he's the best person for the job, then get him here now." Today that CEO is more likely to say, "If he's the best person for the job, then get him on-line now." As globalization increases, knowledge centers begin to have less meaning. True, there are still areas where certain expertise is clustered together—particularly with high-tech industries, dot-com companies, and multimedia companies— but proximity of body is now much less important than proximity of mind. Although it still takes several hours to get a person from the East Coast to the West, an idea can be there in microseconds.

Shared Work

Third, a networked organization also encourages shared work. In traditional organizations, hierarchical divisions often act like impenetrable walls between departments, obstructing access to and exchange of knowledge with others in the same company. Such boundaries also obstruct sharing of work; worse, they can actually result in duplication of work. It makes far more sense—particularly in a time when we never have enough time—to ensure that things only need to be done once.

Shared Decision Making

Because a networked organization is a loose—if tight—collaboration between individual companies or other networking forms, it is obvious that decisions also have to be made with others. This represents a radical change for managers who are used to having the final say. In a traditional organization where there is frequently a customer-supplier relationship—both internally and externally—the customer, who gives orders to the supplier, generally makes the decisions. In a partnership—and networks imply partnerships—such a relationship is between peers. The decision-making process must be shared because there are shared objectives. Although decisions can frequently be made based on a strategic point of view, one partner's meat must not become the other's poison! The aim of any network is to ensure that all participants benefit from participating in it, and thus any individual decision must take into account the good of all as well as the good of the individuals.

Shared Responsibility and Trust

With shared decision making comes shared responsibility, accountability, and trust. This may seem logical, but the contrary often proves true: "Don't ask me." "I had nothing to do with it." "I wasn't involved." As we move into zero space—which must be distinguished, as we saw in chapter 9, by zero resistance—such excuses are not only invalid but also time consuming. If objectives and decision making are shared, then all parties involved must accept responsibility for meeting those objectives.

So it all comes down to trust. It is only human to feel more trust in someone you have met frequently than someone you have never met at all. But as networks expand, change, and rotate, personal one-on-one meetings become less and less frequent. In fact, there is often little time for such face-to-face meetings. The challenge in zero space is to engender trust in an environment where personal contact is rare. Trust is essential if a network is to operate efficiently; in fact, a network is unlikely to function at all if the element of trust is absent.

DEVELOPING TRUST

"The glue that holds networks and communities together includes several ingredients, shared interests and shared tasks are among them. Trust is a key ingredient. Shared interests and tasks can help develop trust, but when trust is lacking or has been betrayed, no amount of enthusiasm for a subject or advantage in joint work can hold these collective entities together."[4]

Shared Priorities

Another characteristic of networked organizations is shared timing and issue prioritization. Shared timing is vital when companies are forced to operate in zero time. The window of opportunity—for all members of the network—will only remain open briefly. So it is essential that all recognize the time span dictated by this window of opportunity. Similarly, issues must be prioritized. Again it is the good of the whole that must count.

Shared Rewards

Finally, there must be shared recognition and reward. "All for one and one for all" is the battle cry today. Every part of the network must feel that it is receiving its fair share of the rewards and adequate recognition for the part it plays in achieving success. The situation often encountered in hierarchical organizations where the manager takes the credit and her subordinates take the blame has even less a place in the networked organization than in the bad old days. In a networked organization, all have to feel they are in a win-win situation. That is the network's strength.

LAT Relationships

Often organizations think of themselves as self-sufficient. They throw up walls to discourage the competition, do everything possible to repel invaders—for they may very well be after their secrets!—and at the same time, ensure that nothing goes out that should remain inside. Any new needs are brought in from the outside and the drawbridge is raised once more. All attention is focused within, and only marketing—on very special occasions—ventures out to survey the surrounding landscape.

In contrast, at the very heart of a networked organization must be the realization that openness is a necessity. Interaction and integration of seemingly diverse disciplines, expertise, knowledge, and skills is what gives a networked organization its strength. An almost free flow of knowledge, ideas, and experiences among all people and companies inside the network is essential if there is to be any attempt at sharing—of objectives, benefits, work, or rewards.

As companies move into zero space, they must realize that marriage "till death us do part" is highly improbable. Instead, they will enter into a series of *LAT* relationships—that is, living apart together. And polygamy will no longer be considered reprehensible, at least not in business relationships.

Downsides

We must point out that networks can have a downside too. We already touched on this point when we discussed the issue of trust. The lack of face-to-face contact, the constant pressure, the changing partnerships—all can result in a network becoming a breeding ground for strife. In fact, many observers have noted that the diversity of cultures, the range of specializations, and the need to integrate all can only lead to conflict. It is important to adopt zero-mindedness—forgetting the ways of doing things in the past in which hierarchical considerations weighed heavier than the ultimate good of the whole—and approach the reasons for strife in a positive way. Flexibility from all parties and constant communication are essential ingredients in the creation of a conflict-free network.

Dynamic Relationships: Key to the Networked Organization

The problem with defining a networked organization is that all organizations are networks, but not all organizations are networked organizations. Installing an electronic network and linking everyone together does not create a networked organization. IT may be the facilitator but it is certainly not the creator. According to Wayne E. Baker, professor of organizational behavior and human resource management at the University of Michigan, a networked organization is "characterized by integration across formal boundaries of multiple types of socially important relationships." Such relationships extend in all directions and include such things as task-related communications and informal socializing, advice giving and advice getting, knowledge acquisition and knowledge sharing.[5] What's more, they extend not only horizontally between peers but also vertically between the various layers of management. They extend across boundaries too, whether internal boundaries between departments and areas of authority, or geographic boundaries—for example, when R&D is located on several different continents.

Some observers have tried to distinguish between "thick" networked organizations—such as those we describe here—and "thin" ones. Thin networked organizations rely on IT; they connect people but do not allow the vertical and social networking that typifies the true networked organization.

There is a story about two men who worked at Philips Electronics research labs. One day, in front of the coffee machine, they began to talk. At the time, one was working in the audio division, the other in video. The man in video said that he was well on the way to developing a laser-based disc that would be used for video. "I just hope management sees the light," he said. The other man thought about it and then said: "I wonder if it would help if they *heard* the light." And that chance meeting was the origin of the development of the compact disc.

Almost every company can tell a similar story. Every time, informal contacts lead to an important new product or technology. Informal contacts—at the coffee machine, at the water cooler, even in the rest room—are common in corporate culture. Yet although they are praised when they take place, they are seldom encouraged. And with the advent of networks such chance meetings are in danger of no longer taking place, especially because many (net)workers now work anytime, anyplace, anywhere, and thus have fewer opportunities for coincidental social contact.

THE ART OF STORYTELLING

Stories convey the norms, values and attitudes, and behaviors that define social groups more fully—with more rounded context—than any other kind of communication. Sharing knowledge of story events—showing by example what happened rather than merely presenting a list of lessons—draws people together. As Jean-Luc Godard said, "Sometimes reality is too complex. Stories give it form."

Unlike cafés and pubs, organizations are not natural habitats for storytelling. Most people in organizations are far too busy appearing to be busy to be able to engage in storytelling. Few organizations create spontaneous storytelling cultures. Yet there is storytelling going on in organizations, and some organizational stories are good stories.[6]

Basically, a networked organization is characterized by a set of dynamic relationships—which thus can change as required—that are customer-oriented. As market demands change, the network needs to expand or contract to provide exactly the services and products that the market demands. Complementary knowledge, expertise, and skills are the essential characteristics of a truly dynamic network. If an organization tries to do everything with the people and knowledge it has in-house, then there can be no talk of a network or, we believe, of sustainable growth and success.

Obviously, however, success cannot be left to chance. An organization's network partners must be identified and chosen with care. For this, managers must be honest in identifying what is missing in the network and understand the type of partner required to provide the necessary expertise. But knowledge and expertise alone cannot decide the perfect network partner; managers must also consider the partner's culture and whether a match can be achieved with the other partners in the network. In addition, they must think about the ability of the potential partner to get up to speed. Working in zero time means there is no room for lengthy discussions or long periods of time to get familiar with the situation. Indeed, the aim should be to achieve an instant synergy between all members of the network so as to ensure that the immediate problem is solved and full advantage is taken of the window of opportunity. Many such decisions will of necessity be to acquire a specific competence—a technology skill, or a logistics skill, or a financing skill.

Decisions about an appropriate partner also require detailed understanding of emerging market demands and a comprehensive understanding of the competence that is missing. In some cases there may be only one possible partner—and then managers will find themselves in competition with others, all eager to acquire that particular competence. In such circumstances the owner of the competence will be looking for a partner that can offer the greatest returns; a win-win situation will be its prerequisite. On other occasions, the competence may be more readily available, and then it is up to the acquiring manager to decide which partner offers the most.

Technology Is Only the Enabler

By now it is clear that a networked organization cannot be achieved through technology alone. Certainly, technology is essential to allow a networked organization to emerge and evolve. But installing a network does not guarantee that the organization will automatically move into the networked era. You do not become a world champion race car driver just by purchasing a Formula 1 car! Still, you wouldn't be allowed on the starting grid without one. This illustrates the common idea that installing a network—or employing a flock of IT specialists—is the key to becoming the sort of networked organization that can prove sustainable in the knowledge-based economy. A network is no guarantee for a networked organization; it is only the enabler.

Perhaps the confusion arises because the same word is used for different things. First, network applies to the technology—the actual information and communication connection between people. Second it refers to a set of organizations, in which partners, suppliers, and customers all have their proper place. It is obvious that although the former can exist without the latter, the latter cannot exist without the former.

But it is exactly at this point that the confusion arises. Many applications designed to assist organizations in their efforts to become "networked" often fail to achieve the change intended. Programs like SAP, PeopleSoft, and Lotus Notes frequently do not meet managers' expectations. Indeed, often these expectations are too great: such applications are expected to achieve a change in both content and context of work. That rarely happens.

Technology itself can never result in the far-reaching changes in behavior and mentality that are essential for moving into zero space. Zero-mindedness—the ability to see things in a new and challenging context without remaining tethered to the old economy—means looking beyond technology at the very premises of doing business. Unless a company can do that, all the networks in the world will simply ensure that its indecision is shared by more people.

Unchained Value

In chapter 6, we already looked at value creation in the zero space organization. The old *value chain* is a relic of the industrial age. It suggests a chain of predictable activities and processes controlled by the company itself. In fact, it reflects the concept of process management—where each link in the chain must look both to supplier and customer—that was developed when traditional functional systems no longer guaranteed customer orientation.

Nowadays, there is no single, clearly defined chain; such linear concepts have no value in zero space. Rather than a value chain there are *value networks*,[7] *digital value*,[8] and *value fields*[9]—the value constellation described in chapter 6. Participating in a network is itself a way to create value because it allows each participant to enjoy advantages and benefits that may not have been possible otherwise. Organizations today have to keep track of an intricate web of relationships—partners, alliances, on-line customers—often in a way so different from the traditional chain that we can truly speak of *unchained value*.

A value network must generate economic value. This driving factor of business will not change, even in zero space! But in a network, this economic value is not generated simply by selling a product that is the result of a process chain. It is the result of a far more complex, and exciting, interaction. It is not a simple trade economy—I sell, you buy—but rather a dynamic interaction between one or more enterprises, customers, suppliers, strategic partners, and the community. Value is created for all members of the chain, thanks to a complex interaction of expertise and benefits. It is generated through the exchange of knowledge and through intangible assets. As we have already stated, what is important is the ability to orchestrate knowledge so that stakeholders in the network can benefit from it. And so we see that the currency of the knowledge-based economy involves three sets of things: goods, services, and revenues; knowledge value; and intangible value (including attention value).[10] Indeed, as more and more products and services depend on the exchange of knowledge and information, intangibles and knowledge will, in themselves, become the currency. Those who think that the value of a networked organization can only be found by looking at its balance sheet are fast losing out in today's reality.

MP3: THE WEB THAT TRAPPED MORE THAN A FLY

The music industry is worth a staggering $38 billion. It is ruled by big names such as CBS, RCA, PolyGram, Sony—all controlling not only record companies but also artists, networks, and distribution channels. For many years, it seemed that the industry was invulnerable. Yes, the occasional artist caused a ripple on the otherwise placid surface, but this was hardly more than a mild disturbance. Vested interests remained complacent in their grip on the industry. And then . . .

And then that seemingly invulnerable industry was brought to its knees by a German invention called *MP3*. Offered in 1991 as a free international technical standard for the compression and distribution of digital audio, it was suddenly discovered in the late 1990s by technically adept young people, who saw in it the potential to build a collection of recordings that would cost a fraction of the price asked by the music industry. The industry watched powerlessly as MP3 made its move across the Web with lightning speed. Suddenly, all you needed was a CD burner in order to compile your own audio collection. In 1998, the music industry lost $10 billion to what it described as piracy. According to authors Don Tapscott, David Ticoll, and Alex Lowy, the success of MP3 is the result of "an Internet-based alliance—a business web—of consumers, businesses (content and software distribution sites like MP3.com, and technology manufacturers like Diamond, maker of the Rio MP3 player), and content providers (musicians)."[11] It is certainly a success that is network-enabled. If there was no Web it is unlikely that MP3 could have had such a devastating impact on music distribution.

The main lesson from the MP3 story, however, is that networking and critical mass can drive change at an incredible speed. Business webs—such as MP3—can generate what Tapscott, Ticoll, and Lowy call *digital capital*. "Digital capital results from the Internet working on three types of knowledge assets: human capital (what people know), customer capital (who you know, and who knows and values you), and structural capital (how what you know is built into your business systems). With Internet working you can gain human capital without owning it, customer capital from complex mutual relationships, and structural capital that builds wealth through new business models."[12] And with all this, you can generate *emotional capital*. Held in the hearts—not the heads—of employees, customers, and other stakeholders, emotional capital is important for creating value and getting attention.

So where *does* value lie in a networked world? Authors Mahanbir Sawhney and David Parikh maintain that many of the upheavals occurring in the business world today find their roots in the nature of intelligence in networks.[13] In the absence of a network, intelligence is stuck; it can be applied only where it lives. If different kinds of intelligence are needed to perform a task, they must all be bundled together in the same place. For instance, a personal computer not connected to a network has to contain all the intelligence needed to process, store, and display information for a wide variety of user tasks. But the nature of the front-end intelligence needed to interact with users is very different from the nature of the back-end intelligence needed to process and store information.

The introduction of networks has bridged the divide between what may be called *back-end intelligence* and *front-end intelligence*. In networks, back-end intelligence can be consolidated and stored on powerful servers, rather than be required by every individual computer. Front-end intelligence can be more specifically designed to meet the user's needs.

Thus, value creation takes on a new dimension. As Sawhney and Parikh point out, "More money can be made in managing interactions than in performing actions."[14]

According to the authors, value is created in a networked world in four main ways:

■ *Value is created at the ends of networks.* The core will contain the generic, back-end intelligence; the peripheries closest to the end user will provide the connections with customers, which is where most value is generated.

■ *Value will result from a common infrastructure.* Again, shared cores of intelligence—both in machine and human networks—will operate as utilities, freeing up companies and people to concentrate on the peripheries where value is generated.

■ *Value will result from increasing modularity.* Companies will move toward offering "plug-and-play" modules of expertise, skills, and competencies. This will have a radical influence on the way they behave. Rather than protecting proprietary knowledge, they will want to spread it around. It may not be long before the concept of *core competencies* will evolve into the concept of distributed competencies.

■ *Value will also result from an ability to orchestrate and conduct.* Companies will want to know where a plug-and-play capability is available. Successful companies and managers will understand that more value can be generated by creating interactions between partners than by performing actions themselves. Acquiring such "plug-and-play" capabilities will be the focus of competitive struggles in the future.

Networking in Zero Space

Networks are an important feature for companies wishing to move into zero space. But they are only that. They are not a guarantee of success; they only provide the foundation on which success can be built.

There is no ideal networked organization. As companies constantly form and regroup, new structures and new organizations will arise in response to each new opportunity. The only networked organizational form acceptable in zero space is the one that provides the best opportunity for creating value.

JUST BREAK UP A WINNING TEAM: EMBRACING RELENTLESS DISCOMFORT

"Leaders in the organization," says Richard Pascale, "keep a careful watch on how teams are performing, and if a team looks like it has moved too far back from the edge of chaos, then senior management will move the team around. They'll pull up some people out of one team and introduce some new people, all for the sake of keeping the creative energy level high. The company's leaders take very seriously the idea of *increasing variety*, both internally and externally: they mix things up internally on their own teams, and they network externally with venture capital firms to look for ideas that they can bring inside."[15]

14

PARTNERSHIPS: RELEASING THE POWER OF UNLIKE MINDS

T HE SECOND ASPECT OF ZERO SPACE ORGANIZATIONS is that they are built on a fluid structure of partnerships. This involves an enormous change in mindset. After all, the corporate mindset has always held that the only way to succeed is to be independent of everyone and everything, to handle the whole industrial chain from A to Z, to leave nothing to chance, to do it all.

This was particularly true of many of the great industrial giants. In the automobile industry, with its revolutionary production line, companies literally did everything from scratch, right down to selling the car to the customer. Many multinationals grew large thanks to their ability to turn in-house innovations into market successes. Own the knowledge, own the technology, own the process: this was the guiding philosophy.

Today, this philosophy is naïve. Knowledge emerges, accumulates, and declines in a matter of months, hours, or even minutes. In this ever-changing world, this is the norm rather than the exception.

As we have seen, zero matter demands a new way of approaching knowledge, skills, and expertise. Don't own it, pluck the benefits from it. The strategic aim of all companies must no longer be to acquire knowledge but rather to ensure access to it anytime, anyplace, anywhere.

Thus, an important competence in zero space is the ability to develop successful partnerships with the appropriate knowledge owners—an ability that we call *partnership IQ*.

Partnership IQ

According to the old point of view, if you have to look for a partnership, then you are making an admission of your company's inadequacy. It signals the market, the competition, and the world that you are not as good as you say you are. It says that your company is both fallible and vulnerable. And anyway, how can you trust partners? Aren't they out to steal your secrets, to use your own knowledge to beat you in the marketplace?

Unfortunately, this attitude is still common in a world where it no longer has validity. It is no longer possible to be a jack-of-all-trades; in fact, it's difficult to be master of even one. The technology—and the range of technologies—in even seemingly mundane products is becoming so extensive that it is no longer a feasible proposition to try to develop things in isolation. Take the electronics in cars, for example. The value of the electronics in cars far exceeds the value of the steel. There are smart ignition systems, smart locking systems, engine management, cruise control, navigation systems. All are becoming standard. Yet it is doubtful that car manufacturers could possibly acquire the chip technology that enables such systems. Partnership is not a matter of choice but a matter of survival.

Yet often there is no actual partnership. Many companies persist in adopting a customer-supplier relationship. They expect to define the services, technologies, or components they require and then receive them at a favorable price. This is no longer a viable proposition in a market where knowledge is highly prized. Partnerships that include comakership, codevelopment, and so on cannot be approached in this way. Companies are beginning to understand that the knowledge and competencies they own *are* their marketable products. It's no longer a buyers' market, it's the knowledge owner who can set prices and conditions.

The Advantages of Partnerships

Obviously, companies don't enter partnerships because it's the fashionable thing to do. There have to be strategic and business advantages to any partnership. In their book *Competing for Partners*, A. P. de Man, H. van der Zee, and D. Geurts list a number of drivers for partnering.[1] Let's look at the main reasons they offer.

Access to New Markets

A partnership can provide access to new domestic and foreign markets. In the old economy, this was a driver for acquisitions—define an area, then discover a company there that offers access to that market. Today, acquisitions are proving less attractive than partnerships.

Increased Efficiency

Partnerships can increase efficiency. Choosing a partner for certain manufacturing and production needs can help reduce costs.

Lower R&D Costs

A partnership can also lower R&D costs. As technology becomes increasingly complex, it makes sense to pool R&D talent and resources, particularly when a partner can offer complementary expertise that is essential for the project but demands a long learning curve.

Worldwide Distribution

A partnership can also offer access to a worldwide distribution organization. This may be more interesting than setting up such a distribution chain from scratch. And of course, if the core competence of a company is not distribution, then why shouldn't it make use of a partner who is a specialist in this area? In many countries, specialized catering operations now serve a large number of hospitals and clinics, freeing those institutions from the need to provide in-house catering facilities and to concentrate, instead, on their core competence: medicine.

New Technologies

A partnership can also allow a company to participate in the development of various—and sometimes competing—technologies. Thus a company can hedge its bets, rather than staking everything on a technology that might not ultimately win the race.

Worldwide Standards

Companies also enter into partnerships to create a worldwide standard. The Philips-Sony partnership for the development of the audio compact disc is an example of this. As the standard is frequently set by the company that is first to market, partnerships can also provide faster access to the market with all the benefits that such speed involves.

The Partnership Inside

It's easy to think of partnerships as a purely external affair. A company enters into a partnership with another company to achieve a competitive edge and create value. Meanwhile, important internal partnerships are often taken for granted. The most fundamental partnership, in fact, is the one between a company and its employees.

Although this is a fundamental partnership in the knowledge-based economy often it is not seen as such. People simply "work for" a company; they are on the payroll and they should be grateful for that.

Such an attitude may have been permissible in the industrial age, when "hands" were hired and fired to suit a company's changing needs. But today that is no longer the case. Knowledge professionals are fully aware of their value, and they expect their employers to understand it too. They—like many in the workforce—now judge a job by the meaning and fulfillment it gives to their lives. They expect to find work satisfying. They expect to be able to have some input into it without running into hierarchical barriers. They want to be part of a company, part of a unit, community, team, or group and to be of value. And they want that value to be recognized in an appropriate way. Not just through a paycheck, but rather through recognition and acknowledgment. If companies treat their employees as partners, then many of these things will automatically fall into place.

The same sort of internal partnership should also be encouraged on a horizontal level. Interdepartmental rivalry causes enormous damage to companies. It is even more insidious when mergers occur and departments of companies with different cultures are integrated. Infighting is often the result.

There may be other negative effects of mergers, and often they come down to the fact that these are not partnerships but rather shotgun weddings. The bride is rushed to the altar before she is fully aware of all the implications of the marriage. Often, companies find themselves in such forced marriages. They have no choice but to deal with the other company, but the relationship is adversarial rather than amicable. And a reluctant partner is worse than no partner at all.

Gauging Your PQ

Partnerships are two-way streets. Just as you would expect your partner to be proactive in the relationship, your own company must be prepared to contribute whole-heartedly as well. For that, companies need to develop PQ—*partnering quotient.*[2]

How can you gauge your PQ? If we examine successful partnering companies, we can devise a list of common characteristics. As you review the list, think about how many of these characteristics you recognize right now.

- *Do you look to the future with a clear vision?* Do you know where you are going? Do you understand which of your company's competencies provide the greatest potential for ongoing sustainability? Are you aware of the complementary competencies required for meeting the new opportunities that present themselves?
- *Do you welcome change?* Are you zero-minded enough to understand that nothing is permanent today, and that change has to be actively embraced rather than feared?
- *Do you creatively resolve conflicts when they arise in your organization?* Are you zero-minded in problem solving? Do you listen to all sides of the story and make a decision that can be accepted by all without so much compromising that the end result is useless?
- *Do you value interdependence more than independence?* Do you encourage sharing rather than keeping things to yourself?
- *Do you take every opportunity to create trust, both through words and actions?* Do you provide an example? Do you generate trust through your own words? Do you encourage everyone in the company to do the same?

■ *Do you openly disclose information and offer feedback?* Do you encourage openness rather than a need-to-know mentality?

Once you have answered all these questions honestly, you will have a good idea of your personal PQ. It is obvious that the more committed to partnership you are as a person—as a manager—the better your chances of generating successful partnerships with other companies.

Characteristics of Good Partnerships

In the old days, partnerships were fairly cut-and-dried affairs. A company looked for a potential partner, made an offer the other couldn't refuse, joined up, and lived happily ever after. Companies sought a partner because of the need for geographical penetration, market accessibility, or greater financial resources, for example. Managers produced a short list of potential partners and then wined, dined, and dated them—with all the risks and heartbreak involved. Ultimately, the need for a partnership was dictated by a need to collaborate in order to achieve a certain strategy.

But now things are different. Time pressure is enormous. Companies cannot afford to enter into long engagements. They need to tie the knot as quickly as possible, and with as many partners as required. As we said earlier, polygamy rules.

There are a large number of partnership issues that need to be addressed—characteristics of the changing attitude toward partnerships in the knowledge-based economy.

They Benefit the Network

First, as we have seen, companies do business with an increasing number of partners. This means that there is less a one-on-one relationship (although, of course, this is still a fundamental), but rather a relationship of partnerships in a network. It also implies that companies do not concentrate solely on individual alliances but rather on partnerships that can *benefit them in their network.* This is a very important difference from the traditional idea of two partners being joined for better or for worse. Today it is a matter of enticing a partner into a network of relationships with the understanding that the relationship will only be for the better—and if it turns out for the worse, then the partnership will be ended in the most friendly manner possible. Managing relationships with each individual partner in an extensive network is a highly demanding task. And few managers have the ability or the background to undertake such a task. It is therefore hardly surprising that many managers feel anxious at the prospect of moving into zero space, because they feel ill-equipped for the challenge. By becoming zero-minded, they take the first step toward increasing their chance for success.

They Are Based on Knowledge Sharing

Second, partnerships today are based on sharing knowledge. But there is a considerable problem here. Many companies simply do not know what they know! So how can they share their knowledge? It is essential that the knowledge present in the company—whether on file or in heads—is compiled, collected, and constantly updated. Only when the full scope of internal knowledge is made visible can a company become an attractive partner. And while one's own company may often be the groom, it will also often be the bride. Understanding the full extent of the knowledge in a company allows its managers to put the proper price on any partnership agreement. If you don't know the full extent of what you have to offer, then you are strategically and economically weaker than you could be.

They Are Based on Complementary Knowledge

Third, most partnerships are formed between "unlike" minds. In fact, we would suggest these are the only sensible forms of partnership. Do you need a partner to reinforce knowledge you already own? Of course not. That would simply mean creating more of the same, whereas today's market requires more of the new and different. Partnerships must be based on complementary knowledge, allowing the two partners to create something together that they could not create individually. Unlike minds: that is the key to success.

But unlike minds imply unlike cultures, unlike working processes, unlike reporting structures, unlike employees, unlike management systems. How do you create unity in disparity? How do you leverage the potential of two or more individual (and individualistic) partners to produce something of creativity and market potential? Here again, zero-mindedness is a fundamental requisite, because it frees the mind of what "should" be or what we are accustomed to and allows us to look at each partnership with a fresh eye and without prejudice.

Thus, a partnership is between unlike minds involved in sharing knowledge and enjoying the mutual benefits arising from and being stimulated by the partnership.

Mergers and Acquisitions

Up to this point we have discussed partnerships in which both parties are interested in sharing knowledge and expertise.[3] But sometimes a company must acquire knowledge in order to gain an edge over the competition. In such cases, managers will frequently reach for a more aggressive weapon: a merger or acquisition. Obviously these differ from partnerships of consent, but if they are to succeed they too need to be based on a solid partnership philosophy. It is important, we feel, to include such partnerships here, because they teach us lessons that can be very valuable in assessing partnerships in general and how they should be handled.

Poor Murphy—he had a pessimistic view on life. Yet he gave us a law that, all too often, seems to hold true: *Anything that can go wrong, will go wrong.* In 1998–99, A. T. Kearney carried out a detailed investigation into 230 merging and acquiring companies, recording their market values and performance figures before and after the merger.[4] Less than a third of them saw an increase in profitability after the merger. Some 14 percent saw no change, and an amazing 57 percent saw a decrease in their postmerger profits.

The top leaders of the companies concerned were then asked a series of questions probing the reasons for the success or failure of the merger. The prime reason for failure was discovered to be that the people involved in mergers and acquisitions were often strangers, thrown together in a joint enterprise, sometimes even against their will.

But there were also other reasons. Let us look at some of them here.

Corporate Fit Put Ahead of Corporate Vision

Fit alone cannot sustain a merger—yet it is frequently given as the reason for that merger. Successful mergers were between companies that placed "vision" before "fit."

Lack of Speed in Installing Leadership

Any leadership vacuum is immediately filled with unnecessary and destructive things: infighting, conflict, unresolved differences, and indecisiveness. Successful mergers had leadership teams in place within one week of the acquisition, the next level of management in place within thirty days, and middle management up and running within ninety days.

Focus on Costs Rather Than Growth

Unsuccessful mergers concentrated on cutting costs rather than on growth. Companies should merge in order to grow—cutting costs is just a defensive mechanism, much like the downsizing exercises of the old economy.

Inward Rather Than Outward Focus

Almost 61 percent of the companies surveyed looked inward for early advantages, cutting jobs, closing factories, and streamlining operations. The result was simmering discontent and growing insecurity in the workforce. Successful mergers looked outward for opportunities.

Corporate Cultural Differences Neglected

The cultural differences—in leadership style, personality, managerial decision making, and communications—caused the greatest difficulties for 70 percent of the mergers investigated. Successful mergers create a new culture that is a sum of the parts. They integrate the best of both worlds to create something greater and better.

Failure to Communicate

A staggering 86 percent of the companies interviewed admitted that they had failed to communicate the merger sufficiently. Good communications can ensure buy-in, both internally and externally. Obviously communications surrounding a merger are complex because of the variety of stakeholders that have to be informed about the operation. But complexity is no excuse for avoidance—and successful mergers paid particular attention to full, open, and detailed communications.

Failure to Manage Risk

It is important for managers to be aware of the need for effective risk management—and install a foolproof system to ensure that risk is not overlooked, something that can seriously jeopardize the chance of success.

One thing successful mergers had in common was that the companies concerned appointed an "integration manager" to guide and direct the operation.[5] This person's job could be likened to that of a shepherd, carefully herding two—or more—flocks into one and ensuring that they did not lose their way as they entered new territories.

Clearing Away Misunderstandings in Partnership Negotiations

Many attempts at creating a partnership fail because of an inability to understand the other. During negotiations, cues and hints are given, and companies use these to assume the "similarities" between the two potential partners. Often a failed partnership is the result of assumed "fit"—and as we have already seen, this kind of fit is not the perfect medicine for a successful partnership. As a recent report demonstrates, the outcome of such negotiations is often a memorandum of *mis*understanding instead of understanding.[6] The following paragraphs describe some potential problems that are caused during partnership negotiations.

Decreased Clarity of Governance Structure

The governance of partnerships often is vague and less clearly defined. This is because shareholders frequently invest in a large number of companies and therefore are involved in a variety of changing partnerships. Often the lack of a single overall strategy makes governance difficult.

Operational Dependence

Ideal partnerships are loose-knit affairs—and many companies prefer this because it allows them to retain a high degree of independence. Problems occur, however, when companies feel that their partner is encroaching on their independence.

Knowledge Intensity

One of the key characteristics of partnerships is a sharing and exchange of knowledge. Yet often companies feel that their proprietary knowledge must be safeguarded. Inevitably, spills of such knowledge occur and it is important to understand exactly who owns and manages the flow. In addition, fundamental research and innovation depend very much on interpersonal relationships. These are particularly difficult to maintain in a flexible network of constantly changing partnerships. Communities—which we will discuss in detail in the next chapter—frequently provide a better means of stimulating such knowledge exchange and interaction.

Different Ways of Judging Value

For one partner, a result may be considered very valuable; for the other, it may have little value. Such disparity of judgment can be largely avoided if the partners share a common vision.

Decline of Social Stability and Commitment

Outsourcing and insourcing have become increasingly frequent as companies concentrate on what they perceive to be their core competencies.

The downside is that there is an increase in the use of temporary employees—and this can seriously affect the company's social stability. In addition, temps are far less committed to a company than permanent employees. Similarly, as networks expand, people are likely to be transferred to other partners in the network, where they experience a different culture and different working methods. Many workers become disoriented as they lose the security of a home base.

Gauging the Corporate Need for PQ

After all we have said here about partnerships, it must be clear that they are not easy things to handle. They require managers to develop a partnership capability that can be just as important as any other management skill. And as the need for partnerships grows, the importance of developing a strong partnership capability increases.

INTEGRATIONAL LEARNING

"Integrational learning is a dedicated set of learning processes concerned with business integration. In order to be effective, both content and process aspects must be addressed. *Content* refers to what must be learned about business integration in order to be able to perform effectively in the new (integrated) situation. *Process* refers to the phasing of business integration, which presupposes a link between corporate and personal change processes."[7]

For small companies with a limited number of reasonably constant partners, there is little need to invest heavily in partnership capability. In contrast, large companies that increasingly depend on an ever-changing network of individual partners need a far more sophisticated capability.

Johan Draulans and Ard-Pieter de Man, at that time both working with KPMG, and Henk Volberda, management and business professor at the Rotterdam School of Management, identified three levels of alliances and partnerships among companies.[8]

At the *basic level* companies do not need extensive partnership capability. Instead they need a basic knowledge of contracting, partnership selection, and ways of monitoring the benefits resulting from the partnership. Such companies should also become members of a community (more on that in chapter 15).

Companies reach the *advanced level* when the scope and amount of their partnerships increases noticeably. Such companies would be advised to standardize the way they select and contract partners. The result will be increasing knowledge of partnerships captured in the corporate memory.

The *highest level* is reached when partnerships become a part of the way the company does business. Partnerships must be constantly initiated, monitored, and evaluated. Complex tools are frequently used for this. Many large companies—such as Microsoft, Philips, Cisco, and Ahold— have reached this level of partnership capability, with programs that allow partners to be classified into certain groups on the basis of a specific set of criteria, such as scope, innovation, knowledge, and so on. In addition, such high-level partnering companies employ a manager to monitor all their partnership activities.

How GE Capital Refreshes Its Corporate Gene Pool

GE Capital Corporation makes a *hundred* small acquisitions a year, deals that it believes refresh its "corporate gene pool." GE follows a consistent pattern: it amplifies survival threats and fosters disequilibrium to evoke fresh ideas and innovative responses.[9]

A Network of Partners

In order to attain competitiveness and sustainability, companies in the knowledge-based economy will ultimately become involved in a network of partners. It is vital to understand the underlying philosophy of both networks and the partners in those networks: it should be a meeting of unlike minds to enable an exchange of knowledge where the issue is not ownership but rather the benefits that can arise from cross-fertilization.

15

COMMUNING INTO
ZERO SPACE

▪ ▪ ▪ ▪ ▪ ▪ ▪ ▪ ▪ ▪

A NEW WORD IS CROPPING UP with ever-increasing frequency in current business jargon. The word is *community*. We are being bombarded with new communities: communities of practice, knowledge communities, communities of commerce, communities of learning, communities of interest, and professional communities. Some people, including Jim Botkin, president of Interclass—a knowledge community of companies in different industries seeking to understand and implement organizational learning—maintain that it is "the next big thing" in organizational theory and practice.[1] Communities weave the organization around knowledge independently of any existing structures. In ten years' time, some predict, communities will be as natural to our concept of organization as teams have become.[2]

With so much attention focusing on communities, one could be forgiven for thinking that the idea is something radically new. In fact, nothing could be further from the truth. The concept of communities has been with us for almost as long as humankind has existed. In the beginning, a community was generally a tribe—a group of people sharing their lives, hunting and cooking together, raising their children together. Tribes grew into village communities, then town communities. People started participating in school communities, local communities, recreational communities.

Although the concept of communities is not new, in business and organizational theory it represents a major and necessary step toward entering zero space.

Distinguishing Between Groups, Teams, Networks, and Communities

One of the problems that managers face today is that many current terms are used for approximately the same idea. There is no clear understanding of why communities are so radically different from the groups and teams that have been around for most of the industrial economy, or the networks that are now emerging. Indeed, if we look at it superficially, we can see how interrelated they all are: teams and groups can belong to networks, networks can belong to communities, communities can belong to networks. And people can belong to all of them—simultaneously!

Groups

As Figure 9 shows, a *group* is generally a collection of individuals who are brought together to deliver a specific product or service or to share information. Groups generally develop as the result of a specific agenda, concentrating on problems that need to be solved. The boundaries are very strict, reporting is hierarchical, and the leadership style is autocratic. The leader maintains control and issues commands to the other members. A group relies on individual performance—all of them doing their best— and in many cases is little more than an assembly of people, each doing a specific job without any real cooperation with the other members. Of course there are dangers in group practices: sometimes they reach consensus and make decisions too superficially and quickly. This kind of "groupthink" largely happens because members don't wish to endanger the sense of cohesion by questioning commonly held, though often unspoken assumptions. Often a group is established as the result of reorganization and remains in existence until the next reorganization.

Teams

A *team* is usually formed to accomplish a specific task. Its members have complementary skills and are selected for inclusion in the team because of these specific skills. Although groups are generally functionally oriented, a team concentrates on the process. Although both a group and a team are

	GROUP	**TEAM**	**NETWORK**	**COMMUNITY**
Purpose	To deliver a specific product or service	To accomplish a specified task	To create and maintain a set of relationships of unlike minds that can act accordingly	To discover value in day-to-day exchanges of information and knowledge
Boundaries	Strict	Permeable	Flexible	Mutually adjusting
Development	Through an agenda of problems that need to be solved	Through a work plan where everybody contributes and the objectives are checked throughout the project	The network will expand and contract according to changes in the environment	On its own, by constantly negotiating its "space." New topics are freely introduced
Members	Members follow reporting hierarchy	Members assigned by senior management	Members join by word-of-mouth	Members join themselves
Leadership style	Autocratic	Benevolent	Disposable	Laissez-faire
Sticky issues	Accountability for results	Responsibility for and commitment to defined common goals	Focus on accountability of members to other members rather than the whole network being accountable to some higher authority	Through trust, with fun and "good vibrations," by passion and commitment
Tricky issues	Groupthink	Failure to recognize and reward team efforts	Loss of control over parts of the business	Can become wrapped up in doing its own thing
Duration	Until the next reorganization	Until the project is completed	Until the network does not renew itself	Until it has servced its purpose

Figure 9. *Differences in Ways of Working*

Source: Based on R. Tissen, D. Andriessen, and F. Lekanne Deprez, *The Knowledge Dividend* (London: Financial Times/Prentice Hall, 2000); R. McDermott, "Learning Across Teams," *Knowledge Management Review*, May-June 1999; E. C. Wenger and W. M. Snyder, "Communities of Practice," *Harvard Business Review*, January-February 2000; S. D. Jones and D. J. Schilling, *Measuring Team Performance* (San Francisco: Jossey-Bass, 2000); D. Cohen and L. Prusak, *In Good Company: How Social Capital Makes Organizations Work* (Boston: Harvard Business School Press, 2001); J. Botkin and C. Seelley, "The Knowledge Management Manifesto," *Knowledge Management Review*, January-February 2001.

multidisciplinary, the former is that by coincidence, the latter by choice. Management generally assigns people to a team, but after that the leadership style is much more benevolent, even though management will check the progress of the team throughout its life and hold the team members collectively accountable for the team's activities and progress. Whereas group members often work independently and without much cooperation, team members are far more complementary in their knowledge and thus build close cooperation with their teammates. On the other hand, team members—because they are all specialists—may be able to appreciate each other's skills but not necessarily understand them. The lack of formal, hierarchical control can sometimes lead to conflict, because team members are unable to control their colleagues or issue commands. At the same time, teams encourage members to use their skills and competencies for the good of all. Failure to recognize and reward team efforts can influence the output of a team effort. Such failure erodes the motivation to go the extra mile. A team generally disbands once its task has been completed.

Networks

A *network* has many of the characteristics of a team, but usually in a more expanded form. It too is based on a meeting of "unlike" minds, but generally takes the form of companies in a mutually beneficial, temporary, and semiformal collaboration. Unlike teams, networks do not necessarily need to meet or even be in the same geographic region. In addition, a network changes with the circumstances—not disbanding when a task has been completed but rather mutating constantly to meet emerging challenges. Team members pool their competencies to work for the common good; network members do the same, but they have a greater awareness of what they can get out of the network relationship than do team members. Team members work to benefit their employer; network members work to benefit both their partners and themselves. There is little hierarchical control because each network member has a high level of independence. Members are accountable to other network members; the whole network is not accountable to a higher authority. The tricky thing about networks is the loss of control over parts of the business and the loyalty of employees.[3] At best there is distributed loyalty of individuals to their own company first, with secondary loyalty to the partner company.

Communities

A *community* has some of the characteristics of each of the previous three groupings, yet is a unique and specific entity. Primarily, a community is a way of communicating with other people who share the same interests, objectives, and purposes. People are not ordered to join a community but rather do so of their own volition. And a community emerges and thrives until it is no longer useful, of interest, or required. It is there because it allows people to communicate with people with whom they have something in common.

For most people, a community becomes something of a home base, where they know they will meet other people and interact. Anyone can become a member, regardless of position, function, or interests. The community's membership is constantly changing—new people join, others leave, new relationships are undertaken and maintained. As new people arrive, new knowledge and information is introduced into the community, where it can be discussed and assimilated. Through this constant discussion, knowledge is more easily shared and acquired than in formal situations. Members feel they are contributing and sharing; they experience it as a two-way process. As members become more familiar with the other members of the community, they become more open, more willing to share. Much of this results from an increased trust in the other members and a growing respect. People start to resonate with each other. But the same thing that makes one person rich can make another person poor. The very cohesion of mutual commitment to a community can become a problem if that makes it clannish and excessively idiosyncratic.

Many communities profit from a facilitator—an individual who guides discussions, looks after archiving the material, and promotes a good community. A facilitator is expected to be a kind of jack-of-all-trades: referee, teacher, helper, counselor, and entertainer—and also to know which role to adopt at any given moment.

On-Line Communities

Today's facilitators can trace their origins back to the very start of on-line communications as we know them. The introduction of the first commercial information services provided one-way communication. Prodigy, Dow Jones, Lexis/Nexis, and CompuServe allowed users to log onto databases and retrieve information. There were also the commercial e-mail services of MCI, Genie, and Bix. All had one thing in common: they were one-to-nothing or one-to-one forms of communication. Later, answering the requests of its users, CompuServe added forums of general and specific interest overseen by professional hosts. This was the start of professional communities. Around 1975, Ward Christensen, the creator of Xmodem, put up the first bulletin board service (CBBS/Chicago) running on an old Altair computer. It was originally intended as a test site for his software, but he soon had people logging on looking for files and answers to technical questions. A sociable sort, Christensen threw the private questions into public view and soon the "techie types" attracted to the site were using it to discuss a whole range of topics. Because Christensen made the code for his BBS public, others soon followed and put up their own systems. Everything was via dial-up, at 1200 baud, and writing was all on-line, so these systems were very local, although it was always likely that someone would dial in from Australia to California just to ask what the weather was like or to look around and see what was happening on the other side of the world.

These local services usually took on the character of the system operator. If that person was a professional, that tended to be the character of the system and the users who were attracted to it. If the system operator was more laid back, then the users tended to set their own tone and gravitate into their own groups, with the techies speaking with the techies, and the social ones going with their own kind.

In the mid-1980s the mail reader was developed and people started doing their reading off-line, downloading a packet of mail, answering it, and then uploading their responses. This phenomenon more than any other caused an explosion in the amount of mail being passed, and system operators (sysops) developed the idea of setting up separate discussion conferences based on a topic.

Around 1987 two sysops who had been swapping files back and forth via their boards expanded that further by echoing mail from one to another using software designated *mail door* and *mail tosser*. This first effort, PCB Echo, truly caused an explosion in the amount of mail moving. The first group, including six sysops stretching from New York to California and Canada, evolved into Interlink, a system that eventually grew to three hundred odd systems covering more than two hundred different topics. In its heyday that network (which later changed its name to ILink) moved 250,000 messages a day, and those small communities became worldwide, with systems in the Far East, Europe, and South Africa, in addition to the United States and Canada.

Suddenly other networks sprung to life, each with its own community culture. Fido was anarchy, with only the loosest of structures. Intelec and SmartNet had very lax admission procedures and thus admitted systems that had technical problems and inexperienced users, all adding to a community culture that probably reflected life more accurately.

With the opening of Usenet to general usage, the sharp decline in computer prices, and services such as AOL, everyone went on-line. What now exists is thus a true reflection of the global community. Of course, who wants to interact with 99 percent of the general population? ILink was described as an oasis of civility in the maelstrom of the general on-line world. Unfortunately, what we mostly see now is that maelstrom, with very few oases of civility left.

Each of these networks, as well as users of various forums of the commercial CompuServe, Usenet news groups, and colleges and private groups, banded together into their own communities. Like kids in a candy store, computer users all over the world dialed in and connected with like-minded others. Local, national, and international boundaries disappeared as connection speeds increased, software became more user-friendly, and costs dropped.

Groups like the Well, a San Francisco–based group that was deeply into ecological issues, sprang up. The Byte Brothers, based in Wichita, Kansas, were totally outrageous. Headed by the late Jimmy Pearson, a legend in his own time, the group was cohosted by a pet rat named Victor. Profanity was required and thin-skinned people were quickly out the door. Cal-Link was dedicated to issues solely Californian. Swiss-Link did the same for issues in Switzerland. The Café Mozart was (and is) home to a group of refugees from lists and network conferences who tired of endless flames and puerile posts and banded together by invitation only to maintain a community to their own liking. Then, and even now, communities existed for almost every topic, with some strictly run, others wide open, anything goes, and all degrees between.

NEW MEDIUM, NEW MEANS OF COMMUNICATION

Because text is a flat medium, it is difficult to express emotion. During live communication, one can see the face of the speaker. Without that aid to interpret a person's words, it is often difficult to understand the tone a writer is using. So shorthand sprung up to enhance on-line messages. To emphasize a point a person could write -underlined- or use a double exclamation point (!!) at the end of a sentence. So-called *emoticons*, including ;) (the smile) or ‹g› (grin), enhance the flat text. TLAs (three letter acronyms) are used as textual shortcuts, often to the point of absurdity. One should not type "rolling on the floor laughing" when ROTFL will suffice. The Byte Brothers introduced PCYLIOHONL (please cross your legs I only have one nail left) around Easter time every year, and recently spun out into the ether from the halls of the Café Mozart has been ISI-HTTYT (I'm Surprised I Have to Tell You This), an all-purpose addition to something that is achingly apparent. (For a fuller list of emoticons and TLAs, look at http://www.freewarehof.org/ acronyms.html.)

Nowadays, it is possible to join Web-based communities dedicated to almost any subject imaginable. Many are e-mail–based, with a server distributing an incoming message to all participants. Moderated lists do the same, except that a moderator reviews, edits, and sometimes rejects messages coming in before distributing them. Yahoo! offers such communities, as do many of the Internet service providers and telephone companies. ICQ claims to be a worldwide community with more than five million participants, although it is debatable whether this is really a community of interest or simply a communication provider.

On-line communities can be interesting, vibrant affairs, with discussion topics constantly changing and new views being expressed. But sometimes they can become exclusive, insular in their outlook. Members know what the others think; the discussion can become routine and flat. The result is waning interest.

Business Communities

Businesses have always had their informal networks—gatherings outside the strict confines of work (for example, networks of expatriates in multinational companies). The annual office party is still the place for managers to prove that they really are human. There are informal networks, often centered round something that binds, such as a network of people who have worked in the same plant or at the same overseas subsidiary. Some large companies even have a network of pensioners.

As IT has penetrated further into organizations, people have built up new networks of relationships. E-mail can be easily exchanged with colleagues—and greatly promote peer-to-peer conversations. E-mail also breaks through hierarchy. It considerably simplifies interaction between people, regardless of their location. It has become the telephone of the knowledge-based economy. With e-mail, several types of business communities have sprung up.

Communities of Interest

E-mail exchanges have resulted in new networks. Often these are informal—e-mail–based versions of watercooler chats. They move onto a higher level when they offer a forum to people who share the same interests. On the Internet, there are *communities of interest* for almost any imaginable subject—music, film, theater, but also Latin grammar, Pokemon cards, classic cars, Leonardo di Caprio, fifteenth-century architecture, and the lost world of Atlantis!

Communities of Practice

The next level is something now commonly referred to as *communities of practice*. These are focused on the exchange of knowledge and information. They could be seen as the knowledge-based economy version of mediaeval guilds. They offer a forum, think tank, guild hall to people operating and working in a clearly prescribed area of expertise. They allow exchange of information among knowledge professionals; they promote sharing. They allow professionals to work easily, universally, inexpensively, and on their own terms. Often such sharing is (electronic) document-based; at other times it is encouraged by a discussion of problems, challenges, solutions, or emerging technologies. Furthermore, communities of practice are becoming a vital element in the creation and maintenance of competencies. Knowledge becomes transparent between people who share the same competencies. What may remain hidden from a supervisor cannot be hidden from colleagues in the same area of technological expertise.

The danger is that a community of practice can become a time-consuming chat group; issues and their discussion can take priority over actual work. For this reason, many communities of practice set themselves clearly defined tasks—for example, how to reduce delivery time to customers by 20 percent.

Communities of Purpose

Finally—and less common or understood—are communities of purpose. These can help create a strategic framework—by agreeing on aims, setting goals, and creating a broad platform on which to build for success. In these types of communities the discipline of the business will pull participants together.

Another benefit of communities can be to provide a forum for customers. Such communities create strong bonds between companies and their customers. Loyalty programs—such as frequent flyer programs— can also provide feedback from the market to ensure that any problems can be discussed between companies and their customers. An open exchange of complaints, views, experiences, and suggestions can be of enormous benefit in creating, strengthening, and maintaining the company-customer relationship.

Intangible Benefits of Communities

Communities offer today's businesses many benefits. First, they can provide the basis for both success and unexpected profits. As synergy is created, unexpected combinations of knowledge may emerge that can in turn lead to new products and services. Second, as companies move out of the old restrictions of time and place, communities can provide everyone— at different levels, each contributing the best—participating in them with a focus that may otherwise be difficult to maintain. Third, because such communities are relatively easy to implement, they can start providing a return on investment almost instantaneously. And fourth, communities provide a comforting feeling, making their introduction relatively uncomplicated. People want a forum in which they can participate and are respected and not taken for granted. Communities can offer the intangible benefit of stimulating a corporate culture that can take the company into the knowledge-based economy.

Companies that have taken the step of creating communities often find they have discovered the key to true wealth: the "hidden gold" that knowledge represents. And companies are being confronted with new potential that probably would have remained uncovered, unexploited in the industrial economy.

Virtual Communities, Zero-Minded Perspective

Take one network, add a mixture of people, connect, shake (but do not stir), and you will have the perfect virtual community that leads to collaborations, supports business objectives, and therefore turns shared knowledge into value.

If only it were that simple.

Communities provide rich collaborative environments for their participants, organizations, customers, and other stakeholders. But one of the biggest challenges in creating a community is being sufficiently zero-minded to look at the subject from a virtual perspective. This is a vital condition—

especially because the creation of a virtual community is one of the first steps in the creation of a zero space organization. Companies cannot afford to make mistakes that will set them off in the wrong direction from the start.

However, there is no ready-made virtual community handbook sitting on the shelf waiting to be taken to the cashier, paid for, and used to instantly install a community like some sort of plug-and-play computer peripheral. Instead, any virtual community that is to afford a company all the benefits possible will need to be tailor-made. And even this is not the correct term. For a virtual community is something organic; it is in a constant state of becoming.

But can people in a community wait for it to take root? We believe they can. People must be given time to become accustomed to being part of a large community. Once a feeling of belonging takes root, then the benefits to the company will be enormous. After all, electronic connections are the fastest, most immediate way of creating the very best match between customer and product or service. It can provide instant reaction to emerging requirements—the dream of any entrepreneur.

However, creating a community does not imply the creation of a knowledge-sharing community. Sharing knowledge in a business context—anytime, anyplace, anywhere—must be the ultimate aim these days. We can only truly enter zero space if we develop ways of sharing the knowledge that is the key to sustainable success. Yet that is the crux of the problem. People don't want to share knowledge.

As we have already discussed, knowledge has always been a way of being "one up" on the competition—whether in private or in business life. Cooks have secret ingredients. We talk of the secret behind a success. People have carefully guarded secrets.

It's the same in the daily business environment. Knowledge has always been compartmentalized. R&D was carefully guarded, customer information was marketing's expertise, the finance department had total control over all payments, customer service corrected faults. The functional organization of the industrial economy actually promoted the creation of secrets.

But organizational structure is not the only thing to foster this secrecy. The "one-upmanship" of knowledge was also—and still is—a key culprit. That, and a feeling of protectionism, combined to persuade employees to keep things to themselves. Certainly in periods where the economy was heading downward, knowing something that could make you invaluable was seen as a way of ensuring your future with a company. If everyone knows everything, then no one is invaluable. If no one is invaluable, then no one is irreplaceable.

Making the Transition to Knowledge Sharing

Making the transition from paper-based company (paper is a wonderful protector of secrets)—through digital paper company—where people print out electronically exchanged documents like veritable electronic Gutenbergs—to a digital knowledge-sharing company cannnot be achieved by issuing a companywide commandment: "Thou shalt share knowledge." Even if that commandment were written in stone and presented to the accompaniment of a bass voice and flashes of lightning, it is doubtful it would achieve its desired aim.

Instead, it is essential to take a number of steps before reaching the final goal. There are, we believe, four important steps, as follows:

Decide with Whom to Share[4]

In practice, there are two types of sharing programs—one for an internal audience, the other for an external audience. Obviously, each has different aims and priorities. Internal sharing programs aim to increase flexibility, efficiency, innovation, and speed. When knowledge is shared it ensures that everybody in the organization is always up to speed. This is a prerequisite for entering zero space.

But so too are external knowledge-sharing programs. Here the emphasis is to provide links with and access to supplier and customer knowledge. Obviously in this age of codevelopment and comanufacture, it is essential that knowledge be shared with suppliers and other partners. But it is equally important that knowledge from the market be accessed instantly to provide input for further innovation and development activities.

Decide What to Share

Here again are two important issues. First, what sort of knowledge should be shared? Second, what should the quality of that knowledge be?

Knowledge to be shared can often extend beyond the best practices that have become an integral part of knowledge-sharing programs. The World Bank, for example, has become a knowledge-sharing institution not only on economic matters but also on information about development gleaned from the many external organizations with which it has links. It has almost adopted the role of a development knowledge clearinghouse!

The quality of the knowledge shared—its value, authenticity, and reliability—is also important. The reputation of companies such as Reuters depends not only on the speed with which they share information with their clients but also on the reliability and accuracy of that information. Many external knowledge-sharing programs recognize this and have explicit guidelines for authentication. Knowledge also needs to be "adapted." Local knowledge—acquired by people on the spot—needs to be adapted for the benefit of the common good; similarly, "universal" knowledge has to be adapted so that it can be effectively applied to a local situation.

Decide How to Share

Again we see a dual strategy adopted by knowledge-sharing programs: the first is often referred to as the *brain drain*—collecting all knowledge available—and the other is known as the *brain chain*—ensuring that knowledge is connected and available when needed.

The collection of knowledge involves capturing it and distributing it. Generally this cannot be an unsupervised operation. Knowledge needs to be codified, stored, retrieved, updated, and removed when it is no longer valid. This is the case even when efficient and comprehensive (on-line) knowledge reporting systems are in place. Simply filling a building with books does not turn it into a library! What's more, knowledge must be adapted—as we have already mentioned—to local use. This might mean translating documents of crucial importance into several different languages.

The connection of knowledge is a much more human matter. People own knowledge, and the benefits of connecting them and allowing their accumulated knowledge to resonate can be of considerable benefit to any company. Connecting people who know with people who need to know is challenging, particularly in those cases when people are not aware of what they know or even of what they should know.

Ultimately, the most successful knowledge-sharing programs will combine the benefits of collection and connection in one accessible infrastructure. This accessibility must be given considerable attention when making decisions about any proposed infrastructure. The choice of the most suitable platform is crucial. The aim may be to "Webify" an existing informal system into an all-connecting global network in which all employees, partners, and local communities are linked together, but this can only be achieved if the people using the system have tools that are helpful, relevant, and easy to use. The aim is not simply to connect but to connect people—and release their creative energy and the interactions they can maintain with each other. Only in this way can shared knowledge become powerful—and profitable—knowledge.

Decide to Share

But I've already done that, you may say. We hope so. But like all management decisions, sharing knowledge costs money. It is essential to reserve the necessary financial resources. But it is also essential to invest the time and energy needed to create a community that satisfies a company's expectations of it. And it also essential to make an investment in attention.

HOW ORGANIZATIONAL CULTURE INFLUENCES KNOWLEDGE SHARING

- Culture—and particularly subcultures—shape assumptions about what knowledge is, and hence, which knowledge is worth managing.
- Culture mediates relationships between individual and organizational knowledge.

> ■ Culture creates the context for social interaction that ultimately deter-
> mines how effective an organization can be at creating, sharing, and
> applying knowledge.
> ■ Culture shapes the processes by which new organizational knowl-
> edge—with its accompanying uncertainties—is created, legitimated,
> and distributed.[5]

The organizational structure may need to be redesigned to allow the community to have a full impact. So too will the incentive structure in the organization. Monitoring—preferably by active participation—is essential to ensure that the shared benefits are tracked and ambiguity is kept at a tolerable level.

Determine the Sell-By Date

Knowledge may appear fresh, beneficial, irreplaceable. But it is just as much subject to deterioration as anything else in this life. What is true today may not be true tomorrow. Knowledge is constantly changing. New knowledge often devalues old knowledge. Certainly in the field of technology, today's knowledge may already be out of date. So when setting up any knowledge-sharing community, it is absolutely vital to recognize the need for constant updating, reviews, and deletion of obsolete knowledge.

Some commentators have pointed out the "knowledge decay" factor.[6] It is not only a question of knowing something but also a matter of knowing what you need to know. Obsolete knowledge is just that—obsolete. Any attempt to hold on to such knowledge is an unnecessary use of time that can better be spent gaining knowledge that is relevant to the present moment.

All too often, companies start a knowledge-sharing community from the wrong perspective: they believe that the more knowledge they can obtain and capture, the greater their strength can be. After all, isn't knowledge strength?

The simple answer is yes. And no. Of course it is essential to capture knowledge. But that in itself has little or no intrinsic value. Knowledge is not worth anything unless it is put to use. Knowledge is only a valuable asset if it is used to add value to a company's operations.

Breaking Down Boundaries

We all feel safer when our boundaries are clear, well marked, well established—a place for everything, and everything in its place. Certainly boundaries have their uses. They help keep discussions "on track" and ensure efficiency. They provide mental concepts that help people understand new ideas quickly and easily. And they provide a common vocabulary for discussing and communicating new concepts.

However, many boundaries are no longer facilitating interaction, but preventing it. Boundaries between departments, partners, and employees do not contribute to the exchange of knowledge and ideas that is the fuel of the knowledge-based economy. Boundaries simply have no place in zero space.

With the changes in organizational structure that we discuss in this book, the breaking down of boundaries is happening whether companies like it or not. There are fewer limits between what is inside the company and what is not. The growth in partnerships and networks has had enormous repercussions on boundaries. Borders are becoming blurred. And this can only be for the better. Thinking out of the box means moving into zero space.

BOUNDARIES OF THE FIRM AS A CRUCIAL STRATEGIC ISSUE

"The boundaries of the firm are a central strategic issue, as evidenced both by business history and more topical issues in strategic management (for example, the debate on outsourcing, networking), and that relates directly to issues such as diversification, vertical integration, joint ventures, strategic alliances, and so on. Organizations from an 'economizing perspective' have to choose the right boundaries; if this is not done, the firm may suffer severe transaction and production costs penalties."[7]

So what should companies do to create boundary-breaking behaviors that stimulate new combinations of knowledge into value-adding potential for the company concerned? Three guidelines can help them develop the sort of zero-minded, boundary-breaking mentality they need.[8]

Question Boundaries

Many boundaries exist in a company—some obvious, some hidden. The obvious boundaries should pose few problems to management; they can be attacked head-on. The hidden boundaries are more insidious because they can continue undetected and provide assumptions for decisions and actions that are no longer valid. It is vital that management understand and expose such boundaries. Questioning boundaries is a characteristic of zero-mindedness. This same inquiring mentality must be adopted when assessing many of the concepts discussed in this book. We have mentioned groups—but often groups themselves throw up boundaries. Knowledge groups may be important in a strategic plan, but not if they exclude input from unexpected sources. Even communities can be full of boundaries—between the established members, visitors, and newcomers, or between specialists and generalists and even between various groups of specialists. By its very nature, professional knowledge is flexible, "leaky," and contextual. With any change or transformation in an organization—its mission or strategy—new knowledge boundaries may arise. That, in return, may trigger innovative boundary-breaking behavior.

Bridge Boundaries

Boundaries are often deeply rooted in an organization. Breaking them down means making radical changes to an organization—not easily done overnight. Sometimes, practical considerations have an influence; imagine the difficulty of breaking down the physical boundary between the R&D building on one side of town and the marketing building on the other. Furthermore, as companies begin participating in networks, new boundaries will arise that cannot be breached in a single attack. Many multinationals are faced with boundaries that seem impregnable—product division boundaries, national sales organization boundaries, manufacturing boundaries. Such things cannot be eliminated in a matter of moments, or, indeed, at all.

For this reason, Mahanbir Sawhney and David Parikh suggest connecting people across boundaries—just like building bridges between two banks without eliminating the river.[9] All too often, boundaries continue to exist in the minds of people. Encouraging zero-mindedness will allow them to see over such boundaries and look at what is happening on the other side. Such links depend on human interaction. Understanding each other is not an organizational matter, but a matter of human willingness to see farther than the comfortable confines of a department, group, discipline, or whatever.

Transcend Boundaries

This is the ultimate way to deal with boundaries—rise above them and thus eliminate them altogether. Enter the "boundary busters"—people with a boundary-breaking mentality who demolish walls within and between organizations. All too often, people simply accept boundaries as something there, never to be changed or challenged. But boundaries are there to be broken down.

Creating Communities Without Boundaries

Are you ready to live in a world without boundaries? That is what communities offer. Communities can exist despite any organizational boundaries. They are independent of locality, building, department, group. In a company, a community of interest, practice, or purpose can be instrumental in providing a strong connection that would not otherwise exist.

Internal communities facilitate the exchange of knowledge between people in the same company. Even though it exists outside the organization's hierarchical and physical boundaries, the community can itself provide the structure that a company may need. It is a challenge to align the emerging community organization with that of the tangible organization. Few companies have yet understood how the community can be used to leverage knowledge in an organized way (even though the very concept of a community is one of nonorganization) and that this organization can be transplanted into the tangible organization with considerable benefits. Not least is that the community is available all the time and provides instant access to the company memory. The exchange of knowledge has a beneficial influence on the company IQ.

However, when joint ventures, mergers, partnership deals, and other network-based organizational forms enlarge the existing community, the result is often a hybrid community based on compromise and incompatibility—incompatibility not only of culture and mindset but also of IT infrastructures. Yet a far greater challenge is to ensure that there is a free exchange of knowledge while at the same time core knowledge is not leaked. Legal safeguards have to be put in place, and many participants may feel these are a restriction. A joint venture community can be enormously beneficial for cross-fertilization. Allowing free exchange of ideas within carefully prescribed boundaries is a challenge that few companies have yet undertaken successfully.

It is not surprising that favorable experiences with an internal community should convince companies to embark on creating an external one. Yet often the idea is put into practice without taking into account the various steps that we have already described. There is no community feeling, no common spirit, no desire to participate. So the result is an on-line ghost town that offers nothing of any interest to customers, suppliers, or other participants. "We've built it," people say in surprise, "so why don't they come?"

Despite such bad experiences, the concept of an external on-line community is not losing ground. Companies such as Yahoo! expect to see a further consolidation of community space as more and more companies recognize the importance of having such a community in place. The biggest concern is that participants will become wary of joining a community because of their increasing impermanence. Trusted names in the world of communities, such as Yahoo! and eBay, are likely to capitalize on their reputation as more people are attracted to the possibilities and interaction of communities.

One problem facing companies that operate a community is gauging how successful it really is. Such knowledge is essential in any discussion about whether or not to continue a community and whether its continuance will have beneficial results.

Stacey Bressler and Charles Grantham offer a number of indicators for deciding on the effectiveness and value-generating performance of a community.[10] They include incremental revenue (resulting from additional sales each visit), incremental profitability (change prices overnight and see what happens), growth in number of community members (in absolute numbers and in relationship to the potential size of the market), sustained membership (does the community attract a loyal membership or is there a high turnover), degree of novelty (is there a continuous flow of new ideas, initiatives), rewards for members for outstanding contributions, and analysis of Web traffic moving to and from the site.

Running Communities

Setting up a community and then expecting it to run itself is overly optimistic, even simplistic. A community must be nurtured. Ruth Williams and Joseph Cothrel describe some critical activities that have to be undertaken if the community is to be a success:[11]

Develop Members

A community without members is no community at all. And a community with too few members—or without the occasional infusion of fresh blood—is liable to become inert, self-satisfied, and uninteresting. Constant attention must be given to membership development—not only number of members but also growth of individual members in the community—and this must be done on an ongoing basis. How can you attract new members of the level required? One way is to work with the community leaders (the opinion makers). And one-on-one promotion to potential members should also become an ongoing part of community life.

Manage Assets

A community can develop assets that are of considerable value, yet often they are not appreciated. The assets of a community can include content, whether generated internally or externally; partnerships, with other groups or communities; the knowledge in the community, including the experience of experts; the community infrastructure itself; and the commitment of the community members. It is important for these assets to be managed in the way that all other company assets are managed. Feedback from community members can help ascertain the community assets and also indicate what members consider its most beneficial aspects.

Provide Community Relations

Most members participate in a community in order to interact and communicate with other people. This is true whether the community exists in the real or virtual world. But inevitably conflicts between members can arise—so-called flames in on-line communities. In most cases, the community itself will try to resolve problems between individuals. Communities, on the whole, are self-governing and conflicts are usually solved with the help of other community members or—occasionally—by the intervention of the moderator.

The Future of On-Line Communities

As providers close down, NASDAQ companies take a dive, and unemployment rises in Silicon Valley, virtual communities are evolving. Original populations have moved on, finding a better value proposition elsewhere. Some people have been tempted to prophesy the ultimate and untimely end of communities.

But despite the evidence to the contrary, on-line communities are clearly here to stay. They offer so many benefits that it is highly improbable that they would suddenly cease. Real-life communities flourish, and on-line communities will similarly flourish. The Internet will not go away. The Internet is about communications, and people have never at any time in history stopped wanting to communicate.[12] The Internet has become one of the most potent drivers for business. Yet it has also brought with it something that flies in the face of the way we have always communicated: anonymity. How do you take people at face value when you never see their faces?

Issues of trust, identity, and anonymity are relevant in on-line communities. Words on a screen are the only indication of the person behind those words. Can you trust that person? Are they really who they say they are?

"I don't think that communities can resolve these issues," says Laurence Prusak, executive director of the IBM Institute for Knowledge Management. "People have to get together in the real world. Three organizations I know are studying this: AT&T, Procter & Gamble, and the U.S. Army. At different levels, they have all studied how much so-called face time you need for a community to have coherence. They all felt that people have to actually meet, either once a month or every other month or some such number. Without that, you get entropy. . . . I have yet to hear about a 'community' that has never met and still has coherence. . . . People have to meet to transmit passion."[13]

But at Shell, communities of several thousand professionals deliver results without meeting each other face to face. At Shell, Endal Logan, Andy Boyd, and Brad Vigers—working for the Shell International Exploration and Production (SIEP) program for managing its technical and business knowledge in the company's geographically fragmented, multi-disciplinary framework—explain how the use of storytelling has helped the organization to overcome the barriers it encountered and directed employee expertise to the places it was most needed. Andy Boyd says, "Campfires stories have been around in Shell since its birth and throughout its development as a geographically disparate company. Our initiative to promote new ways of working needed a simple yet credible way of developing the essential mindset for sharing, so the formalization of storytelling in the service of knowledge management seemed logical. Its success guarantees its status as a permanent feature of our knowledge management culture."[14] In 2000, a total of $237 million was saved across the eleven global networks: communities of several thousand professionals using on-line networks, moderated by global facilitators based in every major Shell operating unit around the world, providing peer group advice and practical assistance. In the benchmarking network, analysis and dissemination of results from a series of exploration and production benchmarking studies helped close $200 million worth of identified performance gaps, mainly because sixty best or better business practices were shared throughout the operating unit.

COLLABORATION FATIGUE?

"I could easily wake up every day and find virtually my entire leadership team off at a meeting somewhere around the globe," says Deborah Copeland, the retail unit executive of BP. "While each one of those meetings would benefit the company in some way, there would be hardly anybody left in the office to keep my own business running. In addition, *you risk burning your people out with all this collaboration.*"[15]

Another issue with on-line communities is that people can become addicted to them, addicted to participating in the discussions with little regard for the actual value it has for the organization.

So should management lay down guidelines about use, participation, and matters of discussion? The idea may be tempting, but doing so could erode the foundation of a community. Free exchange and interaction of ideas, opinions, thoughts are the driving force of any successful community. To restrict it is to run the danger of curbing its creativity. A community can, as we have seen, transcend boundaries—particularly the artificial boundaries that often exist within an organization.

To impose organizational boundaries on the community is to negate one of the greatest qualities it can possess. Boundaries can turn communities into an enclave protected from the rest of the organization (and the outside world). These types of communities are often intolerant of outsiders and diversity and slow to respond to drivers for change.[16]

Community practices and organizational processes will always be at odds, particularly in long-established companies. But restricting the free flow of ideas that can be generated by a community in favor of organizational control is never the right thing to do. The conflict between the two poles of willful control and planned anarchy will never be resolved; the best we can do is find a balance. And that balance can only be achieved as we become increasingly zero-minded.

16

INFORMATION TECHNOLOGY: SPIDER OR FLY?

O N-LINE COMMUNITIES offer a powerful way to uncover, exchange, share, and most importantly, leverage the knowledge available throughout an organization. Yet they require considerable investment—not only in the time and energy that running a good community demands but also in the infrastructure that allows the community to operate constantly and without interruption.

Of course, on-line communities would not be possible without information technology. Certainly, IT has had an incredible impact on the way companies do business. Despite its relatively recent origins, the business community would now be lost without all the advantages it offers. While IT isn't everything, little progress will be made without it. E-mail has started replacing the telephone as the main method of information exchange. How many answering machines now contain the message: "I am not available, please leave a message—or send an e-mail to . . ."? E-mail has become the communication tool of choice in many companies. Although busy executives may "forget" to return a telephone call, they seldom hesitate to reply to an e-mail. Six years ago it was rare to see an e-mail address on a business card. Today, those without an e-mail address are out of the loop, disconnected from reality. The Internet has made us impatient people: just one click, that's all it takes. Install a network, an intranet, and enter the promised land.

Yet as technology improves, evolves, and reinvents itself, the ambition of remaining ahead of the game becomes less attainable. How can people keep up when what they ordered yesterday and installed today is already outdated? We drive innovation at such a breakneck speed that we can't keep up ourselves. There is no life cycle, only a death cycle.

Still, a business without IT is no longer possible, or even desirable. And like all necessities it needs to be managed. In fact, it presents one of the greatest challenges today, for if it is managed successfully its potential for adding value is enormous.

A Guided Tour of the Digital Jungle

IT systems are sprouting with a rapidity that reflects the zero time of our present-day economy. Everything is very attractive—but how do businesspeople choose the most suitable system for their specific needs?

Figure 10 describes the five main categories of IT systems: non-Web-enabled systems, Web-enabled systems, Web-designed systems, knowledge management systems, and intelligent systems.[1]

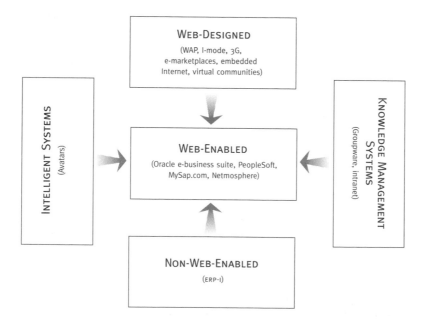

Figure 10. *Categories of IT Systems on the Market*

Source: M. Proos and O. Wiegel, *The Digital Avenue* (master's thesis) (Breukelen, The Netherlands: Nyenrode University).

Non-Web-Enabled Systems

Enterprise resource planning (ERP) belongs quite clearly with the non-Web-enabled IT systems, as do traditional human resource management (HRM) and customer relationship management (CRM) systems. Customer relationship management is an enterprise business strategy to optimize profitability, revenue, and customer satisfaction by organizing the enterprise around customer segments, fostering customer-satisfying behaviors, and linking processes from customers through suppliers. Such systems are non-Web-enabled because they do not use Internet technology or provide a direct link with the Internet. They are based on the client-server model. They can accumulate a wealth of data about a specific subject but are generally stand-alone solutions, providing little connection or linkage with other people or other systems. However, some of these systems—in particular, CRM applications—are being given considerable attention in the business world. Certainly a CRM application can be of vital importance in learning about customer buying behavior and providing a company with input for a new innovation cycle. They are, however, reporting systems only; they do not enable interaction. The new-generation multichannel e-CRM and e-HRM systems are more "Webified." e-CRM is part of broader CRM projects; it can provide additional benefits.[2] e-HRM allows employees self-service, on-line training and career counseling.[3]

Gartner Advisory Services underlines the importance of non-Web-enabled systems by regularly producing an analysis of the market leaders and the shifts they are making.[4] This information is published in what Gartner calls the *magic quadrant* (see Figure 11). We include the magic quadrant here for large manufacturers and distributors—those companies with turnovers in this segment in excess of $800 million—who can use it to evaluate vendors.

Gartner identifies four categories of suppliers: leaders, challengers, niche players, and visionaries. At the moment (2000) Gartner places only SAP and Oracle in the leaders category; SAP thanks its inclusion in this category to its extensive ERP experience, but is likely to lose out to Oracle because the market is not convinced of its e-business capabilities.

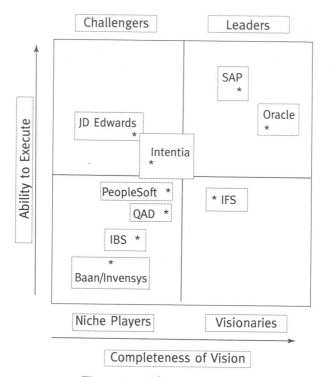

Figure 11. *The Magic Quadrant*

Web-Enabled Systems

Web-enabled systems are likely to be the backbone of companies moving into zero space. Linkage between systems and people are at the core of these systems. The technology is based strongly on the Internet, providing companies with the possibility of linking not only with systems in their own facilities but also with those of partners, stakeholders, and so on. They also provide access to Web-designed facilities such as e-marketplaces. The Internet will become the infrastructure through which companies can link an ever-increasing number of processes, systems, and people with each other. The development of XML is seen by many people as an important step toward an industry-standardized language, which will be essential for enabling interplatform connections. Web-enabled systems will also provide companies with enormous access potential and help lower transaction costs on the Internet.

EXTENSIBLE MARKUP LANGUAGE (XML)

Extensible Markup Language, or XML, is a programming language that has been developed all over the world during the last few years. It is a standardized way of storing raw data (text, spreadsheet numbers, pricing lists, employee records, and so on) so that every number or passage of text carries a little extra information to make it easily identifiable by almost any machine. These "structured data" can be imported and instantly manipulated by software programs and devices that had nothing to do with them in the first place. However, for XML to be truly useful, it must become the standard for storing and shipping data on the Web.

Many suppliers of Web-enabled systems are claiming that they will change the way that business is done. They are calling this new business *collaborative business* or *c-business* and say it is the next e-business trend.

SAP describes how it sees the new c-business: "An employee buying from a Web site creates a purchase order in his or her company's purchasing system and a corresponding sales order in a vendor's order-taking system at the same moment—in one single step. Or two companies jointly use software for collaborative forecasting, which is provided as a service through an electronic marketplace, but integrated with the companies' back-end systems. In each case c-business enhances service while offering new business opportunities, eliminating costs, and ensuring real time satisfaction for all concerned" (see www.sap.com).

Microsoft too is recognizing that the future will be in providing increasingly greater linkage possibilities in Web-based systems. The aim, stated by Bill Gates in June 2000, is "to move beyond today's world of stand-alone Web sites to an Internet of interchangeable components where devices and services can be assembled into cohesive, user-driven experiences."[5]

Several companies are investigating systems that allow managers more up-to-the-moment information than previously. Two such systems are the Net-enabled project management system offered by Netmosphere and a real-time monitoring system offered by Inforay. The latter offers managers an x-ray view of their company at any given moment. It collects, aggregates, and combines the information in various databases across the company or with its partners or suppliers, and presents this in a personalized interface. Thus managers can see what is happening when it is happening, not after it has already happened. As time becomes the essence of business, instant information allows companies to develop fast responses to emerging needs, resulting in increased competitive strength.

Web-enabled systems seem ideal for companies moving into zero space, providing a number of very positive benefits:

- They enable organizations to create unchained value.
- They are independent of time and place through the use of the Internet.
- They enhance value sharing.
- They help companies to speed up processes and response time.
- They offer a uniform platform and can connect various parties.
- They offer a platform for e-business and c-commerce (collaborative commerce).
- They can be personalized to offer user-defined interfaces.

Web-Designed Systems

Whereas Web-enabled systems use the Internet as an infrastructure for linking processes and people together, Web-designed systems are designed explicitly to make use of the Internet. In other words, these services would never have been possible without it. And they are becoming an intrinsic part of the zero space landscape. Let us take a closer look at some of them.

MOBILE E-COMMERCE

The explosion of mobile telephones has resulted in a market penetration that could hardly have been imagined only a few years ago. Here is a brief review of new-generation cellular platforms GSM, GPRS, WAP, 3G, and i-mode.

- *GSM* (global system for mobile communications) allows users to make and receive international calls with a single handset and number. More than half a billion GSM mobile phones are in use globally according to the GSM Association (www.gsmworld.com). This translates to one in twelve people on the planet and means that the technology accounts for more than 70 percent of all handsets. Use is growing at an exponential rate, extending beyond its stronghold in Europe and Asia into the Americas.

- *GPRS* (general packet radio service), or 2.5G, is a new nonvoice value-added service that allows information to be sent and received across a mobile telephone network. It supplements today's circuit-switched data and short message service. GPRS is not related to GPS (the global position system), a similar acronym that is often used in mobile contexts. GPRS will provide a big boost to mobile data usage and usefulness because of its flexible feature set. (See www.gsmworld.com for more information.)

- *WAP* (wireless application protocol) enables mobile devices to display and use wireless applications. It downsizes "fat" graphic-rich Web pages so they mesh with small phone displays. Many European WAP applications have been criticized because of slow transmission speeds and the difficulty of inputting Web and e-mail addresses via a twelve-digit telephone pad.

- With *3G* or *3GSM* (third-generation wireless networks) people will be able to send and receive photos of family and friends, e-mails with moving pictures attached, even the trailer for a new movie. Furthermore, people will be able to experience these while they are on the move. 3GSM will offer high-speed voice, data, and video communications in a single device with a single contact address or number, receiving a person's calls, photos, music, news, and video, with several applications running in parallel if required. (See www.gsmworld.com for more information.)

- Japanese phone company NTT DoCoMo's wireless network technology enables people using an *i-mode* phone to access on-line services, including checking bank balances, making fund transfers, and retrieving information on restaurants or cities, as well as communicate by voice. i-mode employs packet data transmission (9,600 bps); communication fees are based on amount of data sent or received rather than amount of time spent on-line.

One of the newest features is mobile e-commerce. This allows the user to download Internet sites on the mobile phone and use the mobile phone to retrieve information and purchase goods or services. Is this a viable proposition? Research by Forrester (www.forrester.com) shows that the majority of e-commerce will be done over the PC and that the mobile phone will be used mostly to retrieve information and make small purchases, such as tickets. Several technologies—WAP and i-mode, primarily—are aiming to enable mobile e-commerce. The latter is extremely popular in Japan and may travel to Europe but "WAP is dead technology; it is the DOS of the mobile e-commerce world" (conversation with René Tissen, June 2000).

E-Marketplaces

E-marketplaces, or virtual marketplaces, are sites where buyers and sellers can meet on-line to trade. Many virtual marketplaces have emerged, and most try to set the standard for their industry, hoping to reap the greatest profits. Although the actual trading on them remains limited (many are used only for price quotes), the trend has been set. E-marketplaces offer considerable advantages for companies: a worldwide audience and a much larger number of participants independent of time and place. E-marketplaces can save buyers lots of money while sellers gain increased competition.

eBay is an example of a successful e-marketplace. "Some thirty-four million people now participate on eBay, which consists of buyers and sellers from all over the world. Few of them know one another. Nevertheless, they ring up commerce at a staggering rate of nearly $10 billion a year, taking it on faith that someone really will send the money or ship the goods on time."[6]

Virtual Communities of Commerce

There are many kinds of on-line communities of commerce in business, including the following:
- A community of independent resellers sharing tips and ideas.
- A community of buyers and sellers in an Internet marketplace, exchanging information related to purchases or sales
- A community of customers on an Internet commerce site, united by a common interest in topics related to the products offered on the site

▨ A community of people subscribing to an on-line information service, discussing information provided on that service

Members of B2C (business-to-consumers) and B2B (business-to-business) communities of commerce have to prove their value in markets where the customer, armed with more and more information and experiences, uses this "memory" to search out vendors offering the best combination of quality, price, and trust. People are seeking a renewed sense of community and they join on-line communities to find soulmates in the world.[7]

EMBEDDED INTERNET

A relatively new trend is to connect all kinds of electronic appliances to the Internet, making them Web-enabled. An example would be to connect the washing machine to the Internet so that a repair person could diagnose a problem with it from a remote location and make sure he or she brings the right equipment on-site to fix it. We believe there are three options for Web-enabled applications:

▨ *Remote controlling and managing*: controlling the on/off function for emergencies, setting process management parameters, status control, and collecting data.

▨ *Downloading software*: correcting program errors, adapting to the user's demands, selling new software features.

▨ *Intelligent behavior*: using information sources on the Internet, connecting to other embedded systems.

NETWORK-HOSTED APPLICATIONS

The Internet has offered new potential for network-hosted applications, applications a company can lease or rent that are hosted on a network. Companies no longer have to invest heavily in purchasing complete systems and software but can rent the specific applications needed. The next step will be to have the host companies carry out and manage certain processes as well, offering increased flexibility to change processes, add services or products, and reach new markets, without having to finance the necessary investments.

Knowledge Management Systems

Can an IT system manage knowledge? Certainly, although those that claim to manage knowledge today essentially just facilitate the exchange and sharing of knowledge. And that is certainly not the same thing. Groupware and intranet systems provide a link between "owners" of knowledge, but whether they actually encourage people to share knowledge is a different matter.

As shown in Figure 12, Audrey Bollinger, of the Pennsylvania State University, and Robert Smith, of Kent State University, Ohio, have identified many computer-based technologies currently being used to manage knowledge. Apart from infrastructural systems (intranet, extranet, corporate portals) and all kinds of software and database tools to support the codification of explicit and tacit knowledge (knowledge-based systems, lessons learned and best practices databases, data warehouses, yellow pages), the authors distinguish among intelligent tools that anticipate user needs (intelligent agents, advanced search engines) and collaboration tools that facilitate virtual teams and communities (group support systems, distance learning).

Tool Category	Tool
▨ Knowledge infrastructural systems	▨ Intranet ▨ Extranet ▨ Corporate portal
▨ Software and database tools	▨ Knowledge-based systems ▨ Lessons learned and best practices databases ▨ Data warehouses ▨ Yellow pages
▨ Collabaration tools	▨ Group support systems ▨ Videoconferencing ▨ Web conferencing ▨ Distance learning

Figure 12. *Information Technology Tools for Knowledge Management*

Source: A. S. Bollinger and R. W. Smith, "Managing Organizational Knowledge as a Strategic Asset," *Journal of Knowledge Management, 1*, 2001.

Intelligent Systems

Intelligent systems will have an enormous impact on Web-enabled systems and will also be of considerable importance in zero space organizations.

The developers of artificial intelligence are now concentrating on the ability to deal with incorrect or missing information, and to learn from experience. In the future, such software will be able to support manual decision tasks or assume control of them completely.

At the moment, there are three levels of artificial intelligence systems on the market (for more information see www.carp-technologies.nl).

LEVEL ONE: DECISION MAKING BASED ON COMPLETE AND CORRECT INFORMATION

This is the simplest form of artificial intelligence. It takes information, assumes it is correct and complete, and measures it against a set of predetermined rules. The best example is a toaster that releases the toast when it decides it is brown enough.

LEVEL TWO: DECISION MAKING BASED ON INCOMPLETE OR INCORRECT INFORMATION

Such systems can make decisions in a much wider range of situations than those in the previous category. They can predict missing information and correct incorrect information based on their own experiences. One of the applications for such systems is as an interface to allow the user to use conversational English when entering commands.

LEVEL THREE: REFLECTION

This is where we move into what most people would consider to be "true" artificial intelligence. These systems reason and make decisions themselves. Such systems are already in operation, particularly in the field of logistics. Many supermarkets today use them for maintaining stock levels and ordering new stocks to ensure that a predicted demand—based on past consumer buying behavior—can be met. A system will, for example, track the sales of bananas, predict expected demand, and make sure that a minimum stock is maintained without too much waste. The system has to react to a variety of circumstances, such as consumer behavior, holidays, weather, harvest, and trends. It then adapts its internal rules accordingly.

AI systems are also already being used on the Internet. In their more advanced forms, they are able to deal with incomplete or incorrect information, to communicate with other intelligent agents, and to operate independently. They can also trigger the start of a process without the intervention of the user.

VIRTUAL REPS

The virtual representatives (vRep) offered by NativeMinds (www.native-minds.com) understand questions and identify the correct reply. vReps are automated on-line personalities that provide two-way natural-language conversations with customers. A long-term memory retains information about individual Web site visitors from one session to the next, and a conversation database logs conversations between virtual assistants and visitors.

An electronic mailbox answering machine, for example, informs anyone sending an e-mail that the recipient is out of the office. Intelligent agents can trigger a credit card authorization. In the not-too-distant future, they will be able to take over the more mundane tasks of management and employees, freeing humans to spend more time on more complex issues.

It's the People, Not the Technology, That Counts

Although this chapter emphasized the adhesive role of IT in communities, a word of caution is appropriate. It is not the technology that makes a community but the people who participate in it. Installing an electronic network does not create a virtual community, any more than building a community center creates a physical community. Both network and community center are enablers; they can never substitute for the people who are the heart, soul, and mind of the community itself.

Throughout our discussions of IT, we need to ensure that people are given pride of place; doing this will help avoid many of the pitfalls and obstacles that IT can place in our path. Certainly, an organization must be able to ensure that the system encourages all its people to use it and share knowledge with it. It must serve and stimulate, not restrict and rule.

But we must never be tempted to believe that by installing IT we are stimulating an exchange of knowledge. Technology cannot substitute for management. But it can be used to create true collaboration, between people, devices, and applications. The richer the tools available, the more likely people are to search for soulmates, and finding soulmates is at the very heart of communities.

Knowledge is not a commodity. The Internet has not changed that truth, but rather placed it in a new perspective. Libraries made knowledge accessible, but they did not change the intrinsic value of knowledge, either by devaluing it or making it priceless. Today, the Internet is well on its way to becoming an on-line library. Everything is there, but finding it, excavating it from under piles of irrelevance, is becoming more difficult. The old maxim of not knowing everything—but knowing where to find it— is as true today as it has always been.

The search for knowledge and expertise has caused many companies to join networks. Networks are a remarkable way of exchanging expertise and knowledge and offer a win-win situation to all participants. Value is shifting from enterprises that own knowledge to those who know how to orchestrate it.

Is your company ready to join the digital jam session? As we saw in chapter 1 on zero rules, in improvisational jazz the structure supports but does not specify. The structure is there for jazz musicians as a guide, but they investigate the freedoms it offers. This is the way to play the music of success in the knowledge-based economy, too. We must become the ultimate session musicians: ready to pick up a score, take direction, give direction, and play our best at any moment. And we must learn to go with the flow—because cacophony will never attract an interested audience.

There will be a growing number of session musicians. What will make one session more attractive than others? We believe that the extent to which companies conduct business on-line will prove of decisive importance.

Slywotzky and Morrison developed a simple test to help companies ascertain their digital ratio: how much of their key activities are digitally rather than paper-based. We offer the checklist here in Figure 13.

For example, how much of your selling is done on-line? Most companies will check zero to 10 percent. But Charles Schwab does over 50 percent of its business on-line, and Cisco Systems sells more than 90 percent of its products on-line.

Completing the checklist will reveal exactly how many of a business's processes are conducted on-line and to what extent. But it will also provide insight into how far a company has moved along the road to taking full advantage of the possibilities IT offers. As Slywotzky and Morrison clearly indicate, an organization must shift "from a collection of separate silos to an integrated system in which information, ideas, and solutions are shared."[8]

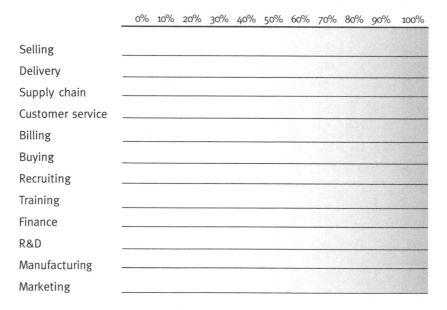

Figure 13. *Determine Your Digital Ratio*

Source: A. J. Slywotzky and D. J. Morrison, *How Digital Is Your Business?* (New York: Crown Business, 2000), p. 16.

Technology is a wonderfully enabling thing in today's world. It allows virtual teams, networks, and communities to share and exchange knowledge. But most importantly, it helps dreams come true, dreams that result when two (unlike) minds connect and share their knowledge. This is what must be encouraged. Technology for the sake of technology is not useful; technology for the sake of dreams is. And although we may be creating artificial intelligence to help us with routine management business, we will never—at least not in the coming decades—create artificial intelligence that can dream.

17

WHAT'S IN STORE?

■ ■ ■ ■ ■ ■ ■ ■ ■ ■ ■ ■ ■ ■ ■ ■

S OME ORGANIZATIONS ARE ALREADY EVOLVING toward zero space. We
see many companies working in zero time with zero matter, forming networks and communities, and enjoying the benefits of knowledge rather than owning it. This is inevitable. Zero space organizations
offer the flexibility that is essential in the face of new—often unpredictable—circumstances. As windows of opportunity increasingly narrow,
organizations will need to be able to adapt swiftly and anticipate the direction in which potential gain and success lie.

Yet although there are signs that some companies are moving into zero
space, it would be inaccurate to suggest that all are moving in the same
direction. Some are actually moving backwards, retracing their past.

This is, perhaps, understandable. Companies and managers today are
under enormous pressure. Shareholders are demanding ever-higher
returns. Managers must try to satisfy the competing claims of shareholders and the other stakeholders who demand "good corporate governance."
Costs are under constant scrutiny. IT promises increased productivity,
which is necessary to defray the investments that IT systems require. Balancing people, planet, and performance is the name of the game. With
increased accountability and transparency, there is greater pressure on
executives to meet targets. In consequence, many are turning back the
clock—and so they centralize and standardize.

The Return of Centralization and Standardization

Over the last fifteen years, many companies have followed a strategy of pushing authority down in the organization. Teams, groups, and business units were all designed to locate both authority and accountability at the place where the work is done. But now, as accountability is being demanded of chief executives, they are once again demanding full control. "If I am expected to carry the show," they argue, "then it is only right that I—together with my team—make the final decisions." Centralize authority. Give the power back to the top.

This reaction to the growing demand for accountability and transparency flies in the face of all we have learned about zero space. How can centralized control exist in a new era of networks and communities, and of enjoying the benefits of knowledge rather than owning it? How can the interaction between individual companies—with their own cultures, strategies, and competencies—be orchestrated if there is complete and total centralized control? Partnerships suggest equality of authority and accountability.

But there is an even greater danger inherent in the demand for accountability: the last few years have seen the rise of smart professionals—people of considerable talent who have been trained to think independently, make decisions, develop capabilities, create order, and operate as they see fit. Are they willing to relinquish control to a centralized power that they often consider to be ignorant of the specific needs of their work and abilities? Will their lack of authority lead to such dissatisfaction that they consider leaving a company altogether? It is a new conundrum: balancing the demands of a new generation of profit-hungry shareholders and stakeholders for good corporate governance with the needs of the people who make the business happen.

In addition to control, pressured executives want standardization. Today's sophisticated IT systems allow for a far-reaching transformation of business procedures. Virtual dependencies between business units and organizations are thought to stimulate responsiveness to customers' demands. Ideally, these "connections" are assembled and disassembled at a moment's notice. IT plays a critical role in extending the company beyond traditional boundaries. But to switch in zero time requires standardization of software, hardware, and "peopleware" (that is, ways to manage people). Often this process results in "fragmented standards," even though the very purpose of standardization is to integrate people's work![1] Organizational life has become far more complex, ambiguous, and unpredictable than it used to be. So standards become standards for today, not necessarily for tomorrow.

Motivations for Centralization and Standardization

Most companies have good reasons for seeking such proven approaches to management. Growth—or rather the constant need for accelerated growth—is yet another driver behind it. Companies that are still facing increased demand (such as Sony with its PlayStation 2) need efficient— and speedy—delivery (certainly in a world ruled by zero time). Standardization, the reasoning goes, can be an important factor in satisfying the increasing demand.

There is also another significant factor in consumer demand: increasing uniformity of taste. Perhaps this uniformity is imposed on the market by companies who see no reason to change "a winning formula." If a Big Mac appeals to people in Arkansas, would not the very same burger appeal to people in Amsterdam, Ankara, or Azerbaijan? We are in the middle of a "brand new world," where shopping malls look the same, products look the same, advertising looks the same, even services look the same.

As long as trade has existed, companies have tried to maintain a balance between costs and supply. What makes the present situation different is that companies are introducing centralization and standardization *simultaneously*. This has far-reaching organizational consequences for any company—but in the world of zero space, the consequences can be devastating.

The most immediate effect of standardization and centralization is that companies will discover they have organized for uniformity. How is this viable in a market where even automobiles—the industry that has done more than anything to define our concept of uniformity and mass production—are subject to such a degree of personal choice that manufacturers are struggling with the challenge of a market that demands mass customization. Doesn't standardization fly in the face of such emerging demand? Would any consumers today allow an automotive company to dictate every aspect of their new car?

The Battle Between Control and Flexibility

When the desire for uniformity conflicts with the need for flexibility it can create harmful tensions throughout an organization. And when companies want to innovate and revitalize themselves, they discover that it is far more difficult to do than they expected. Although culture and tradition may create barriers to the organizational transformation process, there is also resistance from employees. In the past, employees in safe nine-to-five jobs with the prospect of a comfortable retirement may not have wished for authority or empowerment—and certainly not accountability. But today, many employees have enjoyed both, and they are reluctant to return to the old ways. Internal combustion can arise from giving everybody their freedom; it can take on terrifying forms when the organizational transformation requires people to relinquish freedoms they have come to consider their right.

So we are approaching a situation that we call *zero sum employment*. In the industrial economy, people were employed for their manual skills. Determining the productivity of people and monitoring employees was guided by the principle: "Until a human being makes a *motion*, nothing happens." "Hands Wanted" was the sign eagerly sought by people wishing gainful employment. But hands have been superceded by intelligent robots and other computerized tools. Now people search for personnel ads that say "Brains Wanted." Yet both hands and brains are regarded as commodities. Just as hands were expected to repeat the same actions time and time again in the industrial economy, brains are now given the same function in the knowledge-based economy. In fact, today, much knowledge work—brainwork—is as standardized as automobile construction was under Henry Ford. Companies hire human intelligence but employ it as if it were artificial intelligence.

From RSI to RBI?

Repetitive strain injury (RSI) may seem new, but it began during the industrial age when manual routine labor—construction work—caused work-related stress. In the current computer-dominated workplace, RSI has afflicted highly motivated knowledge professionals with a syndrome called mouse arm. But the potential epidemic of the future is repetitive brain injury (RBI)—caused by repeating the same answer over and over again.

Indeed, the situation today shows remarkable parallels with the start of the industrial economy. Today's knowledge-intensive society demands well-educated, well-versed knowledge specialists, but the work of those specialists is becoming routine, standardized. Look at the average customer service department: the training needed to work in such a center—and to answer questions on a whole range of matters—requires a fair amount of knowledge. But the answers these specialists must give are standard, scripted, and documented in detail. They are expected to follow procedures—often known as checklist management—never deviating from the scripts that have been drawn up for them. Ask them something that is not documented and they are lost. So the work is highly information- and knowledge-intensive but at the same time highly standardized. These workers may be using their brains, but they are certainly not required (or even allowed) to use their minds.

Attempts to Standardize Knowledge

So the manual laborer of the industrial economy has become the knowledge worker of the knowledge-based economy.[2] Already, some 80 percent of all knowledge work is standardized.[3] In the financial world, some 43 percent of all transactions take place without human intervention. Just as robots and process automation replaced the need for manual laborers, so the increasing sophistication of IT is replacing the need for knowledge laborers. Knowledge was once considered the ultimate key to success; nowadays it is becoming a commodity like anything else.

This may sound like an exaggeration, but it is not. Knowledge-intensive companies are following the same strategy as their manufacturing forebears. Production once moved to countries offering cheap labor; now companies are moving their facilities to countries offering cheap brains.

The cybersweatshop is a reality. India offers knowledge processing at a fraction of the cost of other countries. Rather than being at the top of the pile, knowledge workers are now at the bottom, taking the place of their manual-labor ancestors. So in light of this emerging situation it is hardly surprising that companies should be reaching for the same strategic tools that proved so effective back then: centralization and standardization.

But there is, of course, a *but*. Today's knowledge workers are far more aware of their own value and employment potential than their forebears were. And it is this awareness that can result in many companies being unable to attract and retain knowledge workers.

Knowledge workers approach work in a different way than traditional workers. They look for jobs that give them satisfaction, inspire them, challenge them.

But standardization of knowledge applications means that knowledge workers are increasingly confronted with procedures, rules, and guidelines. Their position in customer service, as already discussed, is symptomatic of a trend that is gradually affecting large areas of knowledge work. With rules and guidelines come an increasing need for discipline. Knowledge workers are required to follow procedures, whether they like it or not. To ensure that they do, many companies implement far-reaching control systems. Knowledge workers feel restricted, imprisoned in a corporate web of rules and regulations that seem stifling.

So they ask a question: Is there a balance between what I put into this job and what I get out of it? If they ultimately feel that they are putting in far more than they are getting out, they simply up and leave.

The challenge for companies today is to attract, retain, and reward knowledge workers in jobs that are becoming increasingly routine and subject to control. Unless this situation is handled correctly, human resource management can spiral downward into zero sum employment.

Zero Sum Employment and Its Causes

For workers of previous generations, the dream was a job for life. Today, work is seen as a temporary solution to the needs of both employer and employee. Here today, gone tomorrow, seems to be the pervading creed. Companies and employees no longer attempt to give each other the most but rather the least, with the two locked in a tango in which each tries to lower the value of the other. Companies no longer offer employees jobs for life; employees no longer commit themselves to companies. So knowledge workers gain the self-proclaimed freedom to move around from company to company in a sort of corporate musical chairs, and companies move their knowledge work to countries that offer low-cost brain-labor.

A tacit understanding has become part of the negotiation quickstep: knowledge workers silently acknowledge that the company will not get their best, but rather only what the job description specifies, while the company silently acknowledges that the knowledge worker will not receive the best, but rather what the company can get away with. And so companies and workers bargain themselves into mediocrity.

In zero sum employment neither party offers its best to the other. Company and employee do not develop a long-term commitment to each other. Instead, knowledge workers are induced to change jobs frequently and companies move knowledge work to low-cost countries where they have little or no interests. Even in the United States we see the emergence of cybersweatshops. The employees can claim a high level of knowledge, but they are treated with little more respect than factory workers in Victorian times.

Many of the zeroes we have discussed in this book make a positive contribution to companies wishing to move into zero space, but zero sum employment is not one of them. It is a negative and impermanent move that reduces knowledge workers to a menial level. This is, perhaps, logical, because with the "upgrading" of work there is far less work for hands and far more work for brains, and so a new working class has been created at the bottom of the corporate pile. That the people in this category are well educated and intelligent does little to change the attitude of many managers toward the working class.

Other Reasons for Strife Between Worker and Company

In addition to the demands for accountability, good corporate governance, and transparency, all of which put greater and greater demands on managers, other matters too are having an adverse effect on the relationship between knowledge worker and company, and the benefits each can enjoy from the other. We have found four main issues.

Productivity

The demand for standardization can have far-reaching effects on the way knowledge workers are expected to operate. Nonroutine behavior is discouraged; discipline is expected. People are asked to follow carefully prescribed, finely detailed procedures. "If it's not in the book, don't do it." Rules and guidelines proliferate. Freedom to make independent decisions, to think, is ruled out. It is a return to the mechanical, production-line approach of the industrial economy. Do this in twelve seconds and then pass it on. Do not think, just act. And repeat the whole process over again.

The point is to streamline every action so that the highest productivity can be achieved. Any time spent on innovative thinking is wasted.

Indeed, a recent survey showed that no less than 80 percent of U.S. companies of more than a thousand employees are planning to install software whose aim is to monitor employee activity on the Internet.[4] The underlying conviction is that control can result in enormous productivity benefits. Imagine how productive your business would be if you could hold everybody in check and only allow the absolute minimum of freedom. Imagine how much time you would save without all those meetings and all those other communication efforts. This software is able to tell people what to do—without a manager having to lift a finger.

But if a machine is doing *the manager's* job, what will the manager do? That is the question. Who will need departmental meetings? Who will need to waste time explaining procedures, when the system itself will impose these procedures whether one likes them or not?

The idea of total software control is not that far away. Already software is available from Workpace (www.workpace.com) whose aim is to keep computer users healthy. It interrupts work, telling the employee to rest for three minutes, to do some physical exercise, and to relax. Work on the computer is suspended. Once the relaxation period is over, control over the computer, and the work, is returned to the employee.

Until now, of course, people were expected to take charge of their bodies themselves. Most people know when they need to rest, to stretch, to have a cup of coffee or walk around and think. But the procedures that many knowledge workers are expected to follow are so intensive and demanding that many simply forget to listen to their own bodies. And so computers can now do it for them. The procedures today demand such concentration that many workers lose all concept of time, so now the computer that keeps them locked into procedures also takes control over their bodies. Obviously this program has been designed to restrict problems such as eyestrain, carpal tunnel syndrome or mouse arm, and back problems. But the altruistic motives could also be interpreted as an attempt to ensure that every knowledge employee is kept as healthy as possible in order to be as productive as possible.

There is another aspect to this as well. In the struggle to achieve a competitive edge, many companies are rushing to achieve certification. ISO and ITO are today's seals of quality. But the very essence of these standards is—standardization. They are concerned with procedures and how closely a company follows the procedures laid down by some higher institute. ISO and ITO provide the rosaries for today's religion of standardization. We wonder if they really have a place in zero space.

No Room at the Top

Boundaryless careers, career makers, free agents, self-navigators, intraplacement, career agents.[5] Climb the corporate ladder and be master of your own destiny, or someone else will. All these things have become ingrained into the thinking of well-educated and experienced specialists. But the question that must now be asked is: For how long?

As knowledge work moves down the corporate hierarchy to take the place of manual labor, the less bargaining power the knowledge worker will have. There will be less and less room for advancement in an organization. How many manual workers reached the board in the old days? Few. And this will become increasingly true of today's knowledge workers.

For many years, Xanadu was imagined as a place where machines would do the manual labor and people would be free to think. But the real world today suggests that most knowledge work will be repetitive, standardized, and firmly controlled. The passport to paradise is revealed as a one-way ticket to purgatory. Meanwhile, those in charge—management, shareholders, and stakeholders—will get the plum jobs.

Will today's knowledge specialists accept this situation? Will they understand that the more centralized and standardized companies become, the less likely they will be to find true job satisfaction? And will they have a choice? Will they be able to find alternative employment that does satisfy their ambitions and personal desires? We are convinced that those jobs will become few and far between. And there will be zero opportunity.

Just Another Number

Over the last decades individualization has grown. People matter. They are not simply numbers in a corporate or societal environment; they are individuals, with personal needs, ambitions, and desires. Zero space organizations recognize this, paying attention not only to the work but also to the person doing the work.

But this driving force could be totally destroyed—or severely damaged—by the ongoing trends toward centralization and standardization. The danger arises of neglecting the individual—of once again treating people in any but the very top or most highly profiled jobs as numbers. Too much standardization leads to dehumanization. This is what happened during the industrial era, and we are in danger of repeating the same mistake.

But because knowledge workers have been taught to think, question, and search for meaning in their work, they will constantly weigh job security and satisfaction, calculatingly and dispassionately. They will ask themselves where their job is leading, and if it will help them achieve the level of success they demand.

It may seem odd to mention job security here, for we have already discussed how few people see joining a company as a commitment for life. But we must not forget that many of today's employees have witnessed the restructuring and downsizing that had such a drastic effect on the working population. They have become cautious. How do you ensure the continuing commitment and efficiency of those survivors who did not experience "redundancy?" They see companies in the high-tech segment applying the same strategies today. How many dot-com companies have gone belly-up in the recent past? How many have drastically reduced their workforce? Anyone who believes that downsizing and restructuring are a thing of the past has put his head in some very deep sand!

So we see the emergence of the calculating, dispassionate worker we mentioned earlier, constantly gauging the right moment to jump ship. Better to leave before the company asks you to leave.

Furthermore, companies are not particularly disturbed by this trend, although talent retention costs are rising. They recognize that change is inevitable in any business and have come to the conclusion that it is easier to change a company by employing new people rather than people who have become embedded in the company. Long-term employees (survivors), they maintain, are far more resistant to change and will be less malleable in the hands of management. They seem to ignore the fact that any long-term employee has already faced so much change that he or she has learned how to handle it better than others. People employed for a long time by the same company are, in truth, the very model of adaptability.

The Loss of Passion

As we have said, the number of calculating and dispassionate employees is growing. And this lack of passion can have devastating effects on a company. How can an employee be committed to a company, to success, without passion? Standardization, centralization, and the devaluation of knowledge work will result in employees believing they must work with their brains but not their hearts. A committed workforce, once considered an intangible asset of inestimable value, is gradually becoming a corporate myth. The corporate world is becoming rational again. Accountability encourages managers to reach for the weapons of standardization and centralization in their struggle for instant results and higher productivity. Zero space without passion could very well turn out to be a corporate black hole.

The Role of Human Resources

In this ambiguous and unpredictable environment, employees wish that human resources would do anything to get the balance right and make life easier. But the struggle in the jungle of organizational life is hard. Management often (ab)uses this department as a scapegoat. It's nice to have an obedient victim that has the image of being always too late, unresponsive, incompetent, just an extension of the board. Often the HR department is barely surviving in an atmosphere of constant catch-up.

Many human resource management procedures developed in the industrial age. HRM still has a one-size-fits-all approach that flies in the face of the individualization of people and employees. The industrial mindset of many HRM operation systems seems to say: "We think for you and we don't trust you." "People are our most important asset" is placed into a new perspective when downsizing and restructuring show how expendable they really are. And HR departments simply shrug their shoulders and continue business as usual.

But this attitude neglects one fundamental change: when people were simply hands, as replaceable as lightbulbs, their departure meant little to a company. Today, however, when knowledge workers leave they take something with them: knowledge, competencies, and a network. These tools of the knowledge-based economy cannot be checked in when their users leave for employment elsewhere. Even when employees remain with the company, "all your real assets go home at night."

Yet many companies are so stuck in the rut of industrial-age thinking that they cannot appreciate the importance of intangible assets, of which actionable knowledge must be the most intangible, yet the most valuable. How can you appreciate the value of something you cannot see or touch?

As digitization of information and knowledge becomes the rule rather than the exception, managers think they can "see" what is inside people's heads. But they wrongly assume that what is "in the system" is everything they need. As we have already said, zero sum employment means that many employees are giving their employers what is most convenient rather than most of their knowledge.

Zero space organizations will recognize the importance of the tacit knowledge inside their employees' heads and will do everything possible to benefit from it.[6] Thus they will be faced with the challenge of attracting and retaining knowledge partners so that harmony can be achieved between all. Combining knowledge will mean combining talent. And "possessing" digitized knowledge is no guarantee that success will automatically follow. Talent and creativity will be in even greater demand.

Networks will bring together the creative talents of specialists, combining specific capabilities, competencies, and knowledge across borders—anytime, anyplace, anywhere, anyway. But it will be the specialists who are brought together and allowed to resonate and create vibrant work spaces. And this implies that such specialists will essentially specialize in collaboration. True talent will remain something unique; recognizing talent and matching it to the right role will be what drives zero space organizations.

Outsourcing and Insourcing

We've already said it many times: don't own things, enjoy their benefits. And many companies are trying to enjoy the benefits of knowledge by *outsourcing*. In many cases, it is the partner who prefers to offer "talent for hire" rather than "talent for sale." For example, the advertising industry has had a network of freelance specialists for many decades. Many of these specialists enjoy their independence. But the agencies concerned have also profited from the availability of these specialists when they are required, without having to pay overhead when they are not. Photographers, illustrators, copywriters, art directors, stylists, multimedia specialists—all form part of the vast pool of advertising talent. Why own it when you can benefit from it?

THE REEMERGENCE OF GUILDS

"Guilds offer talented workers an organizing principle by which they can associate with others who share an occupational affinity, develop professional skills, and share their need for new ways to provide for benefits and security." Thomas Malone, a professor at MIT's Sloan School of Management, sees that certain organizations are becoming *guildlike*. Staffing agencies such as Aquent, Kelly Services, and Manpower could

> eventually evolve into guilds. Some agencies have been aggressive in
> providing benefits and training as well as attempting to create a sense
> of community, offering a psychological workplace "home" for workers
> who affiliate with them.[7]

Companies wishing to work with zero matter in zero time need instant access to specialists. Long drawn-out selection processes can result in the window of opportunity closing before a team is in place. Today's situation resembles the Hollywood model of staffing: people contribute and collaborate for only as long as the assignment requires. They come together, blending a set of multidisciplinary competencies, focusing on certain parts of the assignment, each at a specific moment, completing the assignment, and then disbanding and moving on to the next one. They develop and share unique intellectual property. They are only as good as their last assignment. They always have to prove themselves.

Outsourcing implies not only that companies know which people to bring in but also that they know where to find them. So it can have its drawbacks. Just as many companies don't know *what* they know, many companies don't know what they *need* to know. And if you don't know that, how do you set about looking for it? Successful outsourcing depends on a high level of internal knowledge. Outsourcing alone is unlikely to be able to handle all the requirements a company will have. Certainly in a time when new combinations of knowledge—plus a pinch of creativity and talent—are at the center of all value-adding activities, companies will need to achieve if they are to remain successful in an ever-more-competitive market.

However, outsourcing is subject to close scrutiny as more realistic cost-benefit analyses reveal fixed costs and a lack of direct control over quality. And there is always the danger of losing customers to the outsourcing partners. ("Why go through them, when you can come direct to me—and save yourself their mark-up?")

Insourcing is often used to expand the internal resources of a company, sometimes even by stealth. Microsoft, for example, distributed thirty thousand free copies of its Windows 98 platform to people throughout the world. Its customers made many suggestions, improvements, and contributions to an almost bug-free Windows 98. In fact, what Microsoft did was insource an enormous group of testers—and it cost the company nothing! If we calculated the sum Microsoft would have had to pay for thirty thousand people, each investing some twenty hours in testing at an average cost of $100 per hour, then the cost would have been around $60 million![8] Furthermore, it's doubtful that Microsoft could have gathered together a group of computer experts willing to work on such a project in any other way.

Finally, one simple question: What will human resources contribute to the zero space organization? Very little, if it does not open itself to change. The changes required are discussed in the next chapter.

MAKING PEOPLE THE NONZEROS OF ZERO SPACE

▪ ▪

H UMAN RESOURCES IS FIRMLY GROUNDED in the industrial organization. For this reason, it must undergo far-reaching changes
if it is to be of any value to the knowledge organization. This is
why many companies are turning to electronic networks on which they
can put all HR-related data, information, services, databases, tools, applications, and transactions.[1] Such information is then available to employees, managers, executives, and HR professionals.

THE EMPLOYEE THUMBPRINT

Launched in April 2000, British Petroleum's myHR.net was jointly designed
and implemented through a partnership with Exult. BP describes it as the
global platform for a human resources service delivery model that links
HR products and services to business objectives by deploying best practices and Web-voice technologies. myHR is branded around several "my"
elements:

- *my Future:* featuring my Profile, my Job Market, and my Learning for
  internal career pathing and development
- *my Agent:* through which e-mail notices of opportunities are matched
  to personal preferences and my Profile
- *my Reward:* a complete, updated view of an individual's compensation-
  benefits package
- *my Data:* self-service maintenance of personal information
- *my Team:* a performance management tool for managers, including
  appraisal, rewards, and reviews

David Latin, global delivery manager of e-HR at BP, says myHR is significant in becoming the employee's *thumbprint* of personalized information, which, when fully rolled out, will be unique to each of one
hundred thousand individuals who work at BP. They will get self-service,
on-line benefits—exactly what they need, wherever they need it.[2]

The New Human Resource Management: On-Line Networks

Will such electronic networks help? That's a difficult question to answer
now. Electronic human resource management is still in its infancy. It
implies shared services and strategic partnerships. Its eventual value could
very well depend on HR people themselves. They must become comfortable with technological change (yes, HR people, so used to telling others
that they must adopt an attitude of flexibility, must now face a major
transformation themselves) and find ways to add value to what is essentially a self-service facility.

Many employees already consider the HR department to be made up
of "faceless individuals"; the introduction of e-HRM may only reinforce
this impression. And HR specialists may begin to wonder if there is any
future for their profession. What can they add to the process when a line
manager or an executive can make direct contact with a potential candi-
date?

Certainly e-HRM can combine the delivery of high-quality HR services with cost savings and process efficiencies. Specialists could work
together in strategic business areas, for example. But many line managers
are reluctant to accept responsibility for HRM even though they are eager
to enjoy the time savings that such systems offer.

Any new technology-based system must be implemented carefully. This
is particularly true with e-HRM. The difficulties largely arise because there
are no clearly defined HR processes. But they will need to be clearly
defined, for automating a mess merely creates an automated mess! The
whole process of HR will need to be rethought.

Managing the Extended Workforce

One of the key challenges will be to manage the extended workforce. An organization's human resources are no longer restricted to its traditional employees. Zero space organizations formally employ only a fraction of the workforce that has relationships with their customers. As Steven Behm, Cisco's former vice president of global alliances said, "At Cisco we have thirty-two thousand employees, but only seventeen thousand of them *work* at Cisco."[3] Indeed, Cisco works with human resources that extend far beyond its corporate boundaries. The company does not out-source functions; it integrates partners. Traditionally, collaboration has been thought of as an activity that occurs inside an organization. The concept of the extended workforce expands collaboration beyond organizational and physical boundaries. A new human resource architecture is needed.[4] We call it *collaborative human resource management* (c-HRM). It achieves dynamic, enterprisewide collaboration among employees, associates, and business partners. It stops the web of collaborations among relevant stakeholders from freezing into fixed patterns, which, once established, are not often revisited. Instead, c-HRM focuses on reconnecting and revitalizing the links among stakeholders.

From Human Resource Management to People Relationship Management

Yet we must never forget that even in zero space organizations, attracting highly qualified employees to a company—and retaining them—will spell the difference between success and failure. *People are our most important resource.* How often have we all read this in the annual reports of companies that consider themselves highly human and people-centered in their outlook. So often, we suspect, that the sentence no longer makes any impact at all.

Yet *resources* are what HRM is all about. Other *RMs* have crept in—notably CRM (customer relationship management)—and these have caused people to take a fresh look at the *RM* in HRM. People in zero space organizations are not resources; to think of them as such shows the narrow-mindedness of a bygone era. The word *resources* suggests things that can be easily replaced—and people ("hands") fell into this category during the industrial economy. But today people have minds of their own, and their knowledge cannot be easily replaced. As we have already discussed, even when elaborate networks are installed to capture knowledge, many areas of knowledge are taken for granted and not entered into a system.

Labeling people as resources indicates an anachronistic way of thinking. In zero space, the individual is the *hub* on which all activities turn. People can make the leap from knowledge to creativity; reducing them to numbers inevitably restricts the creativity that can provide the competitive edge. So we must adopt a new mindset in zero space. Human resource management is out, and people relationship management is in.

Does a name matter? Does this change mean anything at all? We are convinced that it does. The new name reflects a massive change in the whole concept of relationships between people and companies. It is a change that must be encouraged, for it is a change that reveals that a company really is moving into zero space.

In chapter 17 we explained how zero sum employment can have a devastating effect on a company's morale and continuity. At the heart of zero sum employment is a basic indifference to the individual's needs. It is resource management at its worst, a betrayal of the very nature of people: their ability to be creative, to take seemingly unrelated knowledge and fit it together in unsuspected—and often highly profitable—ways. It turns people into something like robots, programmed to repeat the same task over and over again. It exploits their knowledge but fetters their brainpower. It is, ultimately, the recipe for high employee turnover and a stifling of any creative instincts that employees may have.

"Employees are more than resources," says Frans van Veldhoven, a member of the global People Relationship Management (PRM) department of the newly formed Cap Gemini Ernst & Young (CGE&Y). "Nowadays, everybody talks about CRM when they talk about customers; you can't carry on talking about people as 'resources.' PRM is about relationships with people. Those include the present employees, but also past employees and future employees. Traditional HRM only concerns itself with present employees; PRM goes a lot further."[5]

It comes down to understanding that resources are different from assets, and that considering people as resources greatly underestimates their value.

Thomas O. Davenport argues that it is time to take the asset metaphor to a new level.[6] He offers the investor metaphor—workers as investors—to emphasize worker value. However, it also evokes active ideas like building human capital, contributing it to organizations, managing risk, and controlling investments. People possess innate abilities, behaviors, personal energy, and time. According to Davenport, these elements make up human capital—the currency people invest in their jobs. Workers, not organizations, own this human capital. Like financial investors, some human capital investors are more active than others. Viewing workers as investors underscores an essential fact of organizational life—work is a two-way exchange of value, not a one-way exploitation of an asset by its owner.

This was brought home very clearly to the stockholders of Saatchi & Saatchi, one of the world's leading advertising agencies. In December 1994, institutional investors became annoyed at what they considered the arrogant and reckless behavior of the agency's founder and CEO, Maurice Saatchi. In a protracted battle, the investors forced the board of directors to dismiss him. In protest of this action, several top executives resigned from the company, and this was followed by the defection of several major accounts—first Mars, then British Airways. The investors considered all this irrelevant, for it had little or no impact on the balance sheet. But their action backfired: the stock of the agency, which had been trading on the New York Stock Exchange at $8 a share, fell sharply to $4. The shareholders thought they owned the company, but as it turned out they owned only half of it. The other half was human capital—embodied in Maurice Saatchi.[7]

"We are working in two markets," says Pierre Hessler, managing director of CGE&Y, "the business market and the human market. We squeeze sixty thousand brains and hope that some juice comes out that can help our clients solve their problems. Clients are very important to us, but we wouldn't be able to help them without good personnel."[8]

The realization that good personnel are at the heart of the business is something that has not yet filtered through to many layers of the business community. Certainly the professionals' increasingly noncommittal attitude toward companies suggests that they consider themselves less valued than they should be. And this may be the very reason, according to

Hessler, why many professionals no longer consider it attractive to work for a company. "We are entering a period of professional pride," he says. "People want to join a network of professionals to develop their own value. At CGE&Y, we are encouraging this. We have plans for 'communities of practice' where talent, knowledge, and expertise can be developed."[9]

It is interesting that Hessler should mention talent. Often talent is forgotten. When people are considered to be resources, then the aim is to tap into the knowledge they have and transfer it to databases or strictly channel it. The hope is that the database will contain the knowledge that will provide a company with the basis for continuity. But knowledge without talent is of little value. A database could contain every conceivable fact about baseball or soccer, their history, rules, and statistics, but it could never contain the talent to produce a Babe Ruth or a Johan Cruijff. Both baseball and soccer, in fact, understand this better than corporate life: they do not have human resource managers, they have *talent scouts*.

That Cap Gemini Ernst & Young should be so progressive in its thinking may be due in part to the recent amalgamation of the two companies Cap Gemini and Ernst & Young. When this merger was announced, an alarming number of employees left the firm. Nearly a quarter of Ernst & Young's consultants left the company in the months before the merger; at Cap Gemini nearly 20 percent left. Today, after an integration process, employee turnover is low. And the expected culture clash has not occurred; instead, people complain that the name chosen for the new company is too firmly rooted in the past, and efforts are now being made to develop a new name for what is, in fact, a totally new company.

PRM played a vital role in the integration process, and it will continue playing an important role in the future. Professionals working at CGE&Y are expected to contribute to the development of their own professional area. And the way they do this is taken into consideration during wage negotiations.

The advantage of creating a company of communities of practice can be illustrated by the success of the information architecture community. Both Cap Gemini and Ernst & Young had highly trained specialists working in this field; together, they formed a community of practice. Within six weeks, the professionals had drawn up a new, joint vision on architecture and IT strategy. And this is but one of many communities—exactly how many there are is unknown—that have sprung up and continue to spring up in the new company. Many of these begin as what are called "pizza clubs"—people sitting together, eating pizza, and throwing around ideas. Often these clubs tackle very complex problems. Henk Westerloo, global leader of CGE&Y's technology division, reports: "When a club produces a good idea, then it is developed further. If the concept fits in with our plans in the market, then we invest in it. We make use of a growth model for our communities. We encourage them to grow from pizza clubs to full-scale communities with their own events and certification processes."[10]

Communities, talent, ability to share, and wage negotiations based on the extent to which professionals participate and contribute are all methods that CGE&Y is using to get professionals to commit to the company. And people relationship management is given more than lip service. Recently, the entire board of directors dined in Paris with community members who had received their community IT certificates.

A COMMUNITY, NOT A DEPARTMENT

Even in the twenty-first century, human resource functions concentrate resources and activities where they will have the desired business impact. Centralization and decentralization are no longer relevant concepts. Strategies and innovations are increasingly developed in the various business units, in the business context, while central services, such as finance and marketing, focus on providing operational services and support. The function, as a community, embraces all resources providing people-related services, whether they are in the human resources unit or other units (sales training, legal counsel, payroll, and so on) or are provided by external partners or vendors. *The biggest challenge for the human resource staff is getting accustomed to working as a virtual community.* Human resource professionals have been reluctant to rely on vendors or shared services. Once comfortable with resources and controls at hand, they find it difficult to rely instead on influence, collaboration, trust, and shared responsibility. Many will not make this transition.[11]

The Importance of Talent in Zero Space

CGE&Y's experience shows how important talent will be in zero space. But this does not negate the growing awareness that a new class of sweatshop knowledge workers has been created. With the standardization of knowledge activities, talent is now of greater value than knowledge. Knowledge workers may never be able to use their talents; the cream of talent jobs will be skimmed off by those "in control."

Confucius once said: "Choose a job that you like and you will not have to work a day in your life." And common knowledge adds: "A man is a success if he gets up in the morning and gets to bed at night, and in between he does what he wants to do."[12] As we advance into the knowledge economy, our perception of knowledge will change. It will no longer be the key to interesting, inspiring, challenging, and satisfying work; it will become a commodity like anything else. But talent is enduring, and it will be the key to the emergence of worker as investor instead of worker as asset. The talent to combine, to think original thoughts, to create, to innovate—these will increasingly become the key to success in today's turbulent and competitive environment.

KNOWLEDGE EXCHANGE AUCTION

Knexa, the Knowledge Exchange Auction, is a place where users can buy and sell their knowledge and experience on-line. Knexa.com is an on-line knowledge exchange auction site—an arena for people to exchange their specialized expertise, ideas, and discoveries on a vast array of topics. It is a person-to-person as well as business-to-business auction, so prices change based on demand.

As always, the truly challenging jobs will be snapped up by the happy few. In fact, it is not inconceivable that our idea of society will be totally reversed: work—so long the realm of the lower layers of society—may soon belong to a select few. It will become an exclusive club to which talent is the only key.

Attracting talent requires a new mentality, not traditional HR thinking. Talent is individual. If talent is treated like a resource, it will dry up. People relationship management is essential if talent is to be discovered, nurtured, and put to best use.

But this also means that organizations will have to create an attractive environment for such talent. Zero space organizations—based on partnerships, networks, communities, and IT and fueled by talent—contain the seeds of future success.

Let's start the journey.

19

BREAKING FREE

■ ■ ■ ■ ■ ■ ■ ■ ■ ■ ■ ■ ■

WHERE DO YOU GO FROM HERE? What steps should you take? And indeed, how should you take them if the ground on which we are all walking is constantly shifting? How can you mark out a path in quicksand? How can you judge your position when there are no landmarks except those you create yourself? How can we tell you to turn right at the next crossing, when that crossing may very well be here today but gone tomorrow?

Thanks to long experience in the industrial economy, management has learned to go by the book. But there is no book of zero space. Even this present volume can do little more than offer some thoughts for you to take on your journey. It cannot plan the journey for you. For your situation, more than at any time in the past, is unique. And thus your journey will be unique.

Starting the Journey

Still, amid all the uncertainty one thing is certain: the journey must be made. We must approach the eight zeroes of zero space with zero-mind-edness, as well as with curiosity, persistence, and courage. Certainly the fear of failure will surround us. But we must remember that there are only two ways to fail: by not trying and by quitting. All other efforts will be rewarded.[1]

As an old Chinese proverb says, a journey of a thousand miles must begin with a single step. Here are some steps to get your started.

Step 1. Clear Your Mind

The first thing to do is go back to the drawing board. Start observing and behaving in a zero-minded way. Move from single-minded spaces, which fulfill single functions, toward zero-minded spaces, which stimulate engagement and participation with other people.[2]

Zero space organizations, however, cannot be left to chance. They may occur through the constant pairing and rearranging of facts, ideas, choices, alternatives, knowledge, and gossip. But the circumstances in which such events occur need to be orchestrated. They are not routinely present in any of today's model organizations.

The eight zeroes show the conditions that must be in place if a zero space organization will evolve. Basically, it is a matter of mentality. To operate in zero-minded mode means choosing a cut-off point to stop asking questions and seeking additional input, and simply get on with things. If you constantly require fresh data, then you are not operating in zero time. If decisions are reached carefully behind closed doors, then you have not implemented zero exclusion.

So first become zero-minded. Empty your mind of preconceptions. Allow it to move freely where it may never have gone before.

Step 2. Determine Your Zero Space Position

Too often management books suggest that there is only one way to achieve success. In today's fluid and fragmented business world, this is patently untrue. Today, success depends on one thing only: *your* way of doing things. So after you have cleared your mind of all preconceptions, take a good look at your operations and decide how they meet the eight zeroes outlined here.

Figure 14 offers a simple test that will help you determine how your organization currently scores in each of the eight critical zero areas.

Take a key organizational activity and honestly decide how zero spaced it is. For example, are your procurement activities zero spaced? Put the procurement process to the test by asking: Does it work in zero time? Does it offer zero value gap? Does it work with zero exclusion? And so on down the line. Be honest about each characteristic. Based on our experience, most activities get a score higher than 4.

Zero Space	Business as Usual
1	10

Zero Matter	All bricks and mortar
Zero Time	No speed
Zero Value Gap	Take it or leave it
Zero Learning Lag	Learning by accident
Zero Management	Management on top
Zero Resistance	Boundaries, hurdles, barriers
Zero Exclusion	Single minded ownership
Zero Tech	Technology push

Figure 14. *Determine Your Zero Space Position*

This test helps users establish where their company is now, and offers insights into the areas that need work. For example, does your company score an 8 on zero exclusion? Then concentrate on that to create greater potential for the free flow of ideas and sharing of knowledge that is vital for innovative ideas and new combinations of competencies.

PROFITING FROM PERSONAL TO-DO LISTS: SERVING YOUR CUSTOMERS' CUSTOMER

Founded in 1997, Circle Company Associates (www.circles.com) offers Web-based life management: it delivers concierge and personal assistance services to more than eighty companies. By helping customers and employees get their personal errands done, Circle gives them the assistance they need and want, while helping companies achieve their business objectives.

Employers are realizing that today's time crunch takes its toll on employees both on the job and off. Circle's services allow employees to access its Web site from anywhere, anytime. They simply input their personal to-do list, and everything is handled for them.

Katy Sherbrooke, company cofounder, says, "We're trying to provide a full-service application for managing all of the personal tasks in your life, from leisure and luxury all the way down to drudgery and mundanity—settling a bill dispute, waiting for a repairman to show up, or finding a house cleaner." But even this focus on customer relevancy has its drawbacks: While working for Netscape, Lynn Corsiglia, now a vice president of human resources at Dovebid.com.Inc., had access to Les Concierges. "I was working long hours, and, at one point, I had them plan my eldest daughter's birthday party. When my daughter found out, she was furious with me. She thought that I should have done the planning myself. Those services can be helpful, but, if you're not careful, using them can send a wrong message to people in your life."[3]

Circle Company has a responsibility not only to connect consumers and corporate customers to service providers but also to have consumers use the services. For a corporate customer, the greater the percentage of employees who participate and use the services, the more successful the initiative is.

Step 3. Make Zero Space Work

When we consider the eight key characteristics of zero space organizations, we get a balanced sense of cause and effect rather than a focus on one specific feature. Absolute reliability is contrary to human experience. For example, Moshe Rubenstein and Iris Firstenberg show that to demand zero contamination of our beaches, we must first ask what exactly constitutes contamination.[4] We need to establish a numerical consensus describing contamination. Suppose a contaminant is deemed benign at a 10 percent concentration. But we decide to err on the side of caution and allow beaches to remain open only if the contaminant is found in concentrations less than 5 percent. Then we commence cleanup on those that are higher. At this point, some environmentalists may demand removal of the contaminant to zero. The ability to reduce a contaminant from 10 percent to 5 percent is not the same as reducing it from 5 percent to zero. Trying to reach absolutes in any system has a high price, and the benefits may not suffice. The argument is that quantitative measures are almost always preferred to qualitative measures. But quality and quantity go hand in hand; they cannot be separated from each other.

The test will also show you that attention is required across the board. It is highly unlikely that any company will score a 1 in any category. This should not discourage you. Instead, it should urge you to take actions that will eventually lead to improvement. You should not try to reach perfection in one go, but be prepared to make incremental improvements. The most important thing is to get started. Initially you will feel inertia. But once you overcome it, you may well discover that you are moving forward at an accelerating speed. What you must do, however, is get through the inertia as quickly as possible.

Countdown to Zero

In the journey into zero space, the most important ability to develop is zero-mindedness. Be prepared to question everything, to break down ivory towers, to challenge long-held beliefs, to make friends and enemies. And have the courage to make mistakes, for it is better to be a little right than completely wrong.

The journey will be exhilarating, exciting, and fraught with unexpected dangers and obstacles. But it will also be filled with successes, achievements, and that special feeling that comes when you do something that really makes a difference.

Zero space is a challenging approach that effectively supports CEOs, managers, and consultants as they move beyond organizational limits and erase barriers to organizational success. Zero space is a new mindset, one that will help you run your company better. Zero is everything, and everything is zero. You may well discover that entering zero space is the best thing you've ever done for your business.

NOTES

■ ■ ■ ■ ■ ■

PREFACE

1. D. Andriessen and R. Tissen, *Weightless Wealth* (London: Financial Times/ Prentice Hall, 2000), p. 1.

2. T. Stewart, "Note to Bigtime CEOs: Start Thinking Small," *Barely Managing* [www.barely_managing@business2.com], August 2001.

3. S. S. Nim, "Attain Zero Mind, Use Zero Mind," presentation given on May 12, 1978 [www.kwanumzen.com].

4. R. Yeh, K. Pearson, and G. Kozmetsky, *Zero Time* (New York: Wiley, 2000).

5. Yeh, Pearson, and Kozmetsky, *Zero Time*, p. xiv.

INTRODUCTION

1. Even though many dot-coms have failed, they were an innovative experiment that tested radical new ways of starting companies, managing them, and investing in them. In "No One Much Cared" (*Fast Company*, December 2001, p. g2), Tom Peters writes: "Whatever the dot-coms cost us is cheap for the asking. It doesn't matter how much red ink is on the floor. We learned more in the past four years than at any other time in the history of business. You can always print more money, but there's no substitute for getting smarter faster."

2. J. Ellis, "Digital Matters," *Fast Company*, October 2001, p. 82.

3. Mark Levy, *Accidental Genius* (San Francisco: Berrett-Koehler, 2000), p. 4.

CHAPTER 1

1. R. B. Reich, "Your Job Is Change," *Fast Company*, October 2000, p. 144.

2. Reich, "Your Job Is Change," p. 148.

3. Based on S. M. Davis, *2001 Management: Managing the Future Now* (London: Simon & Schuster, 1989); K. Albrecht, *The Northbound Train* (New York: AMACOM, 1994); S. Davis and B. Davidson, *2020 Vision* (New York: Simon & Schuster, 1991).

4. M. J. Hatch, "Exploring the Empty Spaces of Organizing: How Improvisational Jazz Helps Redescribe Organizational Structure," *Organization Studies*, 1999, 20, 75–100.

5. D. Zohar, *Rewiring the Corporate Brain* (San Francisco: Berrett-Koehler, 1997), pp. 37–39.

6. J. Kao, *Jamming* (San Francisco: HarperCollins Business, 1997).

7. J. Ellis, *Doing Business in the Knowledge-Based Economy* (Reading, MA: Addison-Wesley, 1999), p. 174.

8. M. Sawhney and D. Parikh, "Break Your Boundaries," *Business 2.0*, August 2000, p. 34.

9. "But Where Do You Park?" *Fast Company*, April 2001, p. 74.

CHAPTER 2

1. P. Neuhauser, R. Bender, and K. Stromberg, *Culture.com* (New York: Wiley, 2000).

2. T. Stewart, *Intellectual Capital* (New York: Doubleday, 1996).

3. I. Nonaka, H. Takeuchi, and K. Umemoto, "A Theory of Organizational Knowledge Creation," *International Journal of Technology Management, 11* (special issue), 1996, p. 844.

4. I. Nonaka and H. Takeuchi, *The Knowledge-Creating Company* (New York: Oxford University Press, 1995).

5. M. Schrage, "Getting Beyond the Innovation Fetish," *Fortune*, November 13, 2000, p. 5.

6. "Driving Grassroots Growth," *Fortune*, September 4, 2000, pp. 68–70.

7. A. Pendleton, E. Poutsma, J. van Ormeren, and C. Brewster, *Employee Share Ownership and Profit-Sharing in the European Union* (Dublin, Ireland: European Foundation for the Improvement of Living and Working Conditions, 2001).

8. M. M. Crossan, R. E. White, H. W. Lane, and L. Klus, "The Improvising Organization: Where Planning Meets Opportunity," *Organizational Dynamics*, Spring 1996, p. 28.

9. C. O. Scharmer, "Illuminating the Blind Spot of Leadership," presentation at the annual meeting of the Society for Organizational Learning, Ogunquit, Maine, June 2001.

CHAPTER 3

1. M. D. Cohen, J. G. March, and J. P. Olsen, "A Garbage Can Model of Organizational Choice," *Administrative Science Quarterly, 17*, 1972.

2. R. N. Ashkenas, D. Ulrich, C. K. Prahalad, and T. Jick, *The Boundaryless Organization: Breaking the Chains of Organizational Structure* (San Francisco: Jossey-Bass, 1995), p. 3.

CHAPTER 4

1. G. Wolf, "Exploring the Unmaterial World," *Wired*, June 2000, p. 315.

2. Andriessen and Tissen, *Weightless Wealth*, p. 13.

3. A. M. Webber, "New Math for a New Economy," *Fast Company*, January-February 2000.

4. Jeffrey Bezos, "The Company Is Not the Stock," *Business Week*, April 30, 2001, p. 72.

5. W. Sahlman, "In Praise of Irrational Exuberance," *Harvard Business Review*, October 2001, p. 28.

6. Andriessen and Tissen, *Weightless Wealth*.

7. G. Hamel and C. K. Prahalad, *Competing for the Future* (Boston: Harvard Business School Press, 1994).

8. Kevin Kelly, *New Rules for the New Economy* (New York: Viking Penguin, 1998).

CHAPTER 5

1. R. Rodin with C. Hartman, *Free, Perfect, and Now* (New York: Simon & Schuster, 1999).

2. T. A. Stewart, "Three Rules for Managing in the Real-Time Economy," *Fortune*, May 1, 2000, p. 108.

3. G. Imperato, "First Site: Time for Zero Time," *Net Company*, *0001*, 1999, p. 7 [www.fastcompany.com].

4. J. G. Auerbach, "IBM Sees Internet Playing Big Role in Its Future," *Wall Street Journal*, 1999 [www.wsj.com].

5. Neuhauser, Bender, and Stromberg, *Culture.com*, pp. 23–24.

6. J. Rifkin, *The Age of Access* (New York: Jeremy Tarcher/Putman, 2000), p. 22.

7. "Sea of IP," interview with Theo Classen produced for Philips Semiconductors by Jonathan Ellis, Eindhoven, The Netherlands, 2000.

8. D. Tapscott, *The Digital Economy* (New York: McGraw-Hill, 1996).

9. Hein v.d. Zeeuw, "Philips Semiconductors—Partners to the Global Globetrotter," presentation to the Institute of Suppliers to the Semiconductor Industry, 1999.

10. J. Wright and J. Rifkin, "The Age of Access," *Business 2.0*, November 2000 (UK), p. 132.

11. Wright and Rifkin, "Age of Access," p. 132.

12. Yeh, Pearson, and Kozmetsky, *Zero Time*, p. xiv.

13. M. Buckingham and C. Coffman, *First, Break All the Rules* (New York: Simon & Schuster, 1999), p. 33.

CHAPTER 6

1. Yeh, Pearson, and Kozmetsky, *Zero Time*.

2. G. Imperato, "First Site," p. 6.

3. M. Porter, *Competitive Advantage* (New York: Free Press, 1985).

4. M. J. Cronin, *Unchained Value: The New Logic of Digital Business* (Boston: Harvard Business School Press, 2000).

5. O. A. El Sawy, A. Malhotra, S. Gosain, and K. M. Young, "IT-Intensive Value Innovation in the Electronic Economy: Insights from Marshall Industries," *MIS Quarterly*, 1999.

6. B. Pols, "The Innovation Lethargy Cannot Last"("De Innovatie-Lethargie Kan Niet Duren"), *NRC Handelsblad*, January 17, 1997, p. 13.

7. Yeh, Pearson, and Kozmetsky, *Zero Time*, p. 36.

8. W. C. Kim and R. Mauborgne, "Strategy, Value Innovation, and the Knowledge Economy," *Sloan Management Review*, Spring 1999.

CHAPTER 7

1. D. H. Pink, "I'm a Saboteur—Interview with John Taylor Gatto," *Fast Company*, November 2000, p. 244.

2. A. Muoio, "Cisco's Quick Study," *Fast Company*, October 2000, p. 288.

3. G. Imperato, "First Site," p. 6.

4. M. J. Rosenberg, *E-Learning. Strategies for Delivering Knowledge in the Digital Age* (New York: McGraw-Hill, 2001), p. 147.

5. This and all further references to this case are taken from Muoio, "Cisco's Quick Study," pp. 287–295.

6. Yeh, Pearson, and Kozmetsky, *Zero Time*, pp. 105–123.

CHAPTER 8

1. B. Shamir, "Leadership in Boundaryless Organizations: Disposable or Indispensable?" *European Journal of Work and Organizational Psychology*, 8(1), March 1999, p. 53.

2. Shamir, "Leadership."

3. R. Tissen, D. Andriessen, and F. Lekanne Deprez, *The Knowledge Dividend: Creating High-Performance Companies Through Value-Based Knowledge Management* (London: Financial Times/Prentice Hall, 2000).

4. Shamir, "Leadership," p. 56.

5. P. Drucker, "Managing Oneself," *Harvard Business Review*, March-April 1999, p. 74.

6. CEO *Turnover and Job Security* (Boston: Drake Beam Morin, 2000) [www.dbm.com].

CHAPTER 9

1. F. Crawford and R. Mathews, *The Myth of Excellence* (New York: Crown Business, 2001).

2. J. Goldstein, *The Unshackled Organization* (Portland, OR: Productivity Press, 1994).

3. M. E. Raynor and J. L. Bower, "Lead from the Center," *Harvard Business Review*, May 2001.

4. M. Sawhney and D. Parikh, "Where Value Lives in a Networked World," *Harvard Business Review*, January 2001, p. 86.

CHAPTER 10

1. P. M. Senge and G. Carstedt, "Innovating Our Way to the Next Industrial Revolution," *MIT Sloan Management Review*, Winter 2001, p. 24.

2. C. O. Scharmer, "Presensing Emerging Futures: Illuminating the Blind Spot of Leadership," presentation at the annual meeting of the Society for Organizational Learning, Ogunquit, Maine, June 2001.

3. K. M. Eisenhart and D. C. Galunic, "Coevolving: At Last, a Way to Make Synergies Work," *Harvard Business Review*, January-February 2000.

4. M. F. Rubenstein and I. R. Firstenberg, *The Minding Organization. Bring the Future to the Present and Turn Creative Ideas into Business Solutions* (New York: Wiley, 1999).

5. Yeh, Pearson, and Kozmetsky, *Zero Time*, p. 215.

6. Cronin, *Unchained Value*, p. 51.

7. C. Fussler and P. James, *Driving Eco-Innovation* (London: Pitman, 1996), pp. 46–47.

8. Senge and Carstedt, "Innovating Our Way."

9. R. Häcki and J. Lighton, "The Future of the Networked Company," *McKinsey Quarterly*, 2001.

10. J. Weber, "Management Lessons from the Bust," *Business Week*, August 27, 2001, p. 60.

11. R. Lewin and B. Regine, *The Soul at Work* (London: Orion Business Books, 1999).

12. J. F. Moore, "The New Corporate Form." In D. Tapscott, A. Lowy, and D. Ticoll (eds.), *Blueprint to the Digital Economy* (New York: McGraw-Hill, 1998).

13. Lewin and Regine, *Soul at Work*, pp. 59–60.

14. Lewin and Regine, *Soul at Work*, p. 65.

CHAPTER 11

1. L. E. Burbey, "Ubiquitous Internet Computing" [http://ei.cs.vt.edu/www.btb/faa.96/book/chapter24/chp24-01.html].

2. University of Toronto, Canada, 2002; http://about.eyetap.org/fundamentals/.

3. MIT Media Lab, U.S.A., 2002; http://www.media.mit.edu/wearables/.

4. Swiss Federal Insititue of Technology, Wearable Computing Lab, Switzerland, 2002, http://www.wearable.ethz.ch.

5. J. Ellis, *Investing in Responsibility* (Eindhoven, The Netherlands: Global Panel Foundation, 2000).

CHAPTER 12

1. E. Jaques, "In Praise of Hierarchy," *Harvard Business Review*, 1990, pp. 127–128.

2. P. Prelerse and E. Kerkman, "Ex-McKinseyite" ("Ëx-McKinseyanen"), *Financieel Dagblad*, April 19, 2001.

3. S. M. Davis, *2001 Management: Managing the Future Now* (London: Simon & Schuster, 1989).

4. "The Virtual Corporation," *Business Week*, February 8, 1993, p. 41.

5. A. Mowshowitz, "Ethical Dimensions of Information Technology in Global Business." In W. M. Hoffman (ed.), *Ethics and the Multinational Enterprise* (Washington, DC: University Press of America, 1986).

6. A. Mowshowitz, "Virtual Federalism." In P. J. Denning and R. M. Metcalfe (eds.), *Beyond Calculation: The Next Fifty Years of Computing* (New York: Copernicus, 1997), p. 215.

7. J. E. van Aken, L. Hop, and G.J.J. Post, "The Virtual Organization: A Special Mode of Strong Interorganizational Cooperation." In M. C. Hitt, J. E. Ricart, I. Costa, and R. D. Nixon (eds.), *Managing Strategically in an Interconnected World* (Chichester, UK: Wiley, 1998).

8. C. W. Choo, *The Knowing Organization. How Organizations Use Information to Construct Meaning, Create Knowledge, and Make Decisions* (New York: Oxford University Press, 1998), p. 247.

CHAPTER 13

1. N. Nohria and R. G. Eccles (eds.), *Networks and Organizations: Structure, Form, and Action* (Boston: Harvard Business School Press, 1992), p. 4.

2. S. R. Barley, J. Freeman, and R. C. Hybels, "Strategic Alliances in Commercial Biotechnology." In N. Nohria and R. G. Eccles (eds.), *Networks and Organizations: Structure, Form, and Action* (Boston: Harvard Business School Press, 1992), p. 5.

3. J. F. Rockart and J. E. Short, "The Networked Organization and the Management of Interdependence." In M.S.S. Morton (ed.), *The Corporation of the 1990s* (New York: Oxford University Press, 1991), pp. 192–193.

4. D. Cohen and L. Prusak, *In Good Company* (Boston: Harvard Business School Press, 2001), p. 51.

5. W. E. Baker, "The Network Organization in Theory and Practice." In N. Nohria and R. G. Eccles (eds.), *Networks and Organizations: Structure, Form, and Action* (Boston: Harvard Business School Press, 1992), p. 400.

6. Cohen and Prusak, *In Good Company;* Y. Gabriel, *Storytelling in Organizations* (Oxford: Oxford University Press, 2000).

7. C. Jones, W. S. Hesterly, and S. P. Borgatti, "A Global Theory of Network Governance: Exchange Conditions and Social Mechanisms," *Academy of Management Review*, 1997.

8. G. Hamel, *Leading the Revolution* (Boston: Harvard Business School Press, 2000).

9. This phrase was coined by Kees Linse, COO, Basell NV. For more on this see chapter 6.

10. T. H. Davenport and J. C. Beck, *The Attention Economy: Understanding the New Currency of Business* (Boston: Harvard Business School Press, 2001).

11. D. Tapscott, D. Ticoll, and A. Lowy, *Digital Capital—Harnessing the Power of Business Webs* (Boston: Harvard Business School Press, 2000), pp. 4–5.

12. Tapscott, Ticoll, and Lowy, *Digital Capital*, p. 5.

13. Sawhney and Parikh, "Where Value Lives."

14. Sawhney and Parikh, "Where Value Lives," p. 82.

15. A. M. Webber, "How Business Is a Lot Like Life," *Fast Company*, April 2001, p. 134.

CHAPTER 14

1. A. P. de Man, H. van der Zee, and D. Geurts, *Competing for Partners* (Amsterdam: Prentice Hall, 2000).

2. S. M. Dent, *Partnering Intelligence* (Palo Alto, CA: Davies-Black, 2000).

3. O. Gupta and G. Roos, "Mergers and Acquisitions Through an Intellectual Capital Perspective," *Journal of Intellectual Capital*, 2, 2001.

4. A. T. Kearney, "The Seven Deadly Sins of Post-Merger Integration," *Executive Agenda*, *III*(1), second quarter, 2000.

5. R. N. Ashkenas and S. C. Francis, "Integration Managers: Special Leaders for Special Times," *Harvard Business Review*, November-December 2000.

6. *1+1=3. Managing International Partnerships and Alliances: An EFQM Benchmarking Study Project* (Brussels: European Foundation for Quality Management, 2001).

7. J. C. Bakker and J. W. A. Helmink, *Successfully Integrating Two Businesses* (Aldershot, UK: Gower, 2000), p. 155.

8. J. Draulans, A. P. de Man, and H. Volberda, "Alliance Capability: A Source of Competitive Advantage" ("Alliantievaardigheid: Een Bron Van Concurrentievoordeel"), *Holland/Belgium Management Review*, *16*(63), January-February 1999.

9. Webber, "How Business."

CHAPTER 15

1. J. Chatzkel, "A Conversation with Jim Botkin, President of Interclass," *Journal of Intellectual Capital*, *1*(3), 2000.

2. E. Wenger, "e-Speed, Strategy, Learning, and Community in the E-conomy," presentation made at Interclass meeting [www.interclass.com], November 2001.

3. Thanks to Ronald J. van Solt, Senior Vice President, Strategy and Planning, Royal Ahold, for bringing up the idea that networks can be "tricky."

4. World Bank, *Knowledge for Development* (Oxford, UK: Oxford University Press, 1998).

5. D. W. de Long and L. Fahey, "Diagnosing Cultural Barriers to Knowledge Management," *Academy of Management Executive*, *14*, 2000, pp. 125–126.

6. Neuhauser, Bender, and Stromberg, *Culture.com*.

7. N. J. Foss, "The Boundary School: Strategy as a Boundary Decision." In H. W. Volbeda and T. Elfring (eds.), *Rethinking Strategy* (London: Sage, 2001), p. 114.

8. Foss, "The Boundary School."

9. Sawhney and Parikh, "Break Your Boundaries."

10. S. E. Bressler and C. E. Grantham, *Communities of Commerce* (New York: McGraw-Hill, 2000).

11. R. L. Williams and J. Cothrel, "Four Smart Ways to Run Online Communities," *Sloan Management Review*, 41, 2000.

12. M. J. Mandel and R. W. Hof, "Rethinking the Internet," *Business Week*, March 26, 2001.

13. "How Virtual Communities Enhance Knowledge," an interview with L. Prusak and B. Kogut [Knowledge@Wharton], December 2001.

14. E. Logan, "A Pipeline for Collaboration Leveraging Knowledge Through Storytelling at SIEP," *Knowledge Management*, December 2001/January 2002, p. 33.

15. M. T. Hansen and B. von Oetinger, "Introducing T-Shaped Managers: Knowledge Management's Next Generation," *Harvard Business Review*, March 2001, p. 115.

16. A. Kleiner, "The Tyranny of Community," *Strategy & Business*, 2000.

CHAPTER 16

1. This section was adapted from M. Proos and O. Wiegel, *The Digital Avenue* (master's thesis) (Breukelen, The Netherlands: Nyenrode University, 2000).

2. "An Eagle Eye on Customers," *Business Week*, February 21, 2000.

3. C. Ashton, *e-HR: Transforming the HR Function* (London: Business Intelligence, 2001).

4. Gartner Advisory Services, "Large Manufacturer/ Distributor ERP Magic Quadrant," *Research Note Markets*, June 21, 2000.

5. "Microsoft Will Spend $2 Billion Between 2000 and 2003 to Allow Partners and Developers to Create Microsoft Net Sources," *Newsbytes News Network*, June 22, 2000.

6. G. Anders, "eBay Learns to Trust Again," *Fast Company*, December 2001, p. 104.

7. J. Cothrel, "Measuring the Success of an Online Community" [www.participate.com], October 2001.

8. A. J. Slywotzky and D. J. Morrison, *How Digital Is Your Business* (New York: Crown Business, 2000), p. 18.

CHAPTER 17

1. N. Dean Meyer, *Decentralization. Fantasies, Failings, and Fundamentals* (Ridgefield, CT: N. Dean Meyer and Associates, 1998).

2. P. F. Drucker, "Knowledge-Worker Productivity: The Biggest Challenge," *California Management Review*, 41(2), Winter 1999.

3. Tissen, Andriessen, and Deprez, *The Knowledge Dividend*, p. 69.

4. A. van der Ziel, "Every Click Is Registered" ("Elke Klik Wordt Geregistreerd"), *FEM*, November 27, 1999.

5. M. Arthur and D. Rousseau, *The Boundaryless Career: A New Employment Principle for a New Organizational Era* (New York: Oxford University Press, 1996); the concept of the self-navigator was developed by Edwin Reijntjes, Partner NMC Group, Amsterdam; J. Sullivan, Intraplacement (San Francisco: San Francisco State University, Human Resource Management College of Business, 1998).

6. T. Haldin-Herrgard, "Difficulties in Diffusion of Tacit Knowledge in Organizations," *Journal of Intellectual Capital*, *1*(4), 2000; G. Von Krogh, K. Ichijo, and I. Nonaka, *Enabling Knowledge Creation: How to Unlock the Mystery of Tacit Knowledge and Release the Power of Innovation* (Oxford: Oxford University Press, 2000).

7. J. Rosenfeld, "Free Agents in the Olde World," *Fast Company*, May 2001, p. 138.

8. Our thanks to M. Schrage, codirector of MIT's Media Labs eMarkets Initiative.

CHAPTER 18

1. C. Ashton, *e-HR: Transforming the HR Function* (London: Business Intelligence, 2001).

2. Ashton, *e-HR*, p. 116.

3. Tapscott, Ticoll, and Lowy, *Digital Capital*, p. 170.

4. D. P. Lepak and S. A. Snell, "The Human Resource Architecture: Toward a Theory of Human Capital Allocation and Development," *Academy of Management Review*, 24(1) 1999.

5. "CGE&Y Does Not Employ 'Resources'" ("Bij CGEY Werken Geen 'Resources'") *De Automatiseringsgids*, March 23, 2001, p. 25.

6. T. O. Davenport, *Human Capital* (San Francisco: Jossey-Bass, 1999).

7. T. A. Stewart, "Brain Power: Who Owns It and How They Profit from It," *Fortune*, March 17, 1997.

8. "CGE&Y," p. 25.

9. "CGE&Y," p. 25.

10. "CGE&Y," p. 25.

11. J. W. Walker, "Perspectives" [www.walkergroup.com], February 2001.

12. E. Weber, *The Wisdom of Business* (London: Orion Business Books, 1998), p. 207, p. 212.

CHAPTER 19

1. A. Mortell, *The Courage to Fail* (New York: McGraw-Hill, 1993).

2. R. Rogers, *Cities for a Small Planet* (London: Faber and Faber, 1997).

3. T. Schwartz, "What If You Turned Over Your Uncompleted Wish List to Someone Else?" *Fast Company*, July 2000, p. 298, 300.

4. Rubenstein and Firstenberg, *The Minding Organization*.

INDEX

ABOUT THE AUTHORS

■ ■ ■ ■ ■ ■ ■ ■ ■ ■ ■ ■ ■ ■ ■ ■ ■ ■ ■ ■

Frank Lekanne Deprez is senior consultant at KPMG Knowledge Advisory Services and part-time associate professor at the Universities of Professional Education Zuyd, Heerlen, The Netherlands. He advises national and international organizations on operational and strategic knowledge management and business integration issues and on creating vibrant virtual communities. His passion is helping organizations target and apply knowledge when and where it is really needed.

Before joining KPMG, Lekanne Deprez was a research associate at Tilburg University and held management and functional positions at Royal Dutch Airlines (KLM). From 1995 to 1997, he was manager of market and product development at Galileo Nederland, Ltd. He is coauthor of *Value-Based Knowledge Management* (1998) and *The Knowledge Dividend* (2000).

René Tissen is managing director of KPMG Knowledge Advisory Services and professor of business management at the School of Business at Nyenrode University, The Netherlands. As an international consultant and researcher, he specializes in advising companies on boardroom-level matters involving knowledge management, organization, and human resource management. Previously, he held a number of executive and senior management positions in Dutch industry and government, as well as positions abroad.

René Tissen is coauthor of *Value-Based Knowledge Management* (1998), *The Knowledge Dividend* (2000), *Weightless Wealth* (2000), *Telling IT Like IT Is* (2002), and *Seven Deadly Sins of Management* (2002).

Berrett-Koehler Publishers

BERRETT-KOEHLER is an independent publisher of books, periodicals, and other publications at the leading edge of new thinking and innovative practice on work, business, management, leadership, stewardship, career development, human resources, entrepreneurship, and global sustainability.

Since the company's founding in 1992, we have been committed to supporting the movement toward a more enlightened world of work by publishing books, periodicals, and other publications that help us to integrate our values with our work and work lives, and to create more humane and effective organizations.

We have chosen to focus on the areas of work, business, and organizations, because these are central elements in many people's lives today. Furthermore, the work world is going through tumultuous changes, from the decline of job security to the rise of new structures for organizing people and work. We believe that change is needed at all levels—individual, organizational, community, and global—and our publications address each of these levels.

We seek to create new lenses for understanding organizations, to legitimize topics that people care deeply about but that current business orthodoxy censors or considers secondary to bottom-line concerns, and to uncover new meaning, means, and ends for our work and work lives.

See next page for other publications
from Berrett-Koehler

Leadership and the New Science
Discovering Order in a Chaotic World
2nd Edition, Revised and Expanded

Margaret J. Wheatley

In a completely revised and updated edition of her bestselling classic, Margaret Wheatley shows how the "New Science"—the revolutionary discoveries in quantum physics, chaos theory, and biology that are overturning centuries-old models of science—provides powerful insights for transforming how we design, lead, and manage organizations.

Paperback, 215 pages • ISBN 1-57675-119-8 • Item #51198-406 $18.95

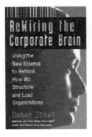

Rewiring the Corporate Brain
Using the New Science to Rethink How We Structure and Lead Organizations

Danah Zohar

Drawing on a solid background in the contemporary sciences, *Rewiring the Corporate Brain* details the ways in which organizational structures mirror the organization of the human brain, shows how to utilize the capacity of the whole corporate brain, and describes a fundamentally new conceptual model for deep transformational change to the structure and leadership of organizations.

Hardcover, 250 pages • ISBN 1-57675-022-1 • Item #50221-406 $27.95

Imaginization
New Mindsets for Seeing, Organizing, and Managing

Gareth Morgan

"Imaginization" is a way of thinking and organizing. It is a key managerial skill that will help you develop your creative potential and find innovative solutions to difficult problems. It answers the call for more creative forms of organization and management. *Imaginization* shows how to put this approach into practice.

Paperback, 350 pages • ISBN 1-57675-026-4 • Item #50264-406 $19.95

Berrett-Koehler Publishers
PO Box 565, Williston, VT 05495-9900
Call toll-free! **800-929-2929** 7 am-12 midnight
Or fax your order to 802-864-7627
For fastest service order online: **www.bkconnection.com**